FIRST TIME
PLANTING

FIRST TIME PLANTING

GAY SEARCH
AND
GEOFF HAMILTON

BBC BOOKS

Published by BBC Books,
a division of BBC Enterprises Limited,
Woodlands, 80 Wood Lane, London W12 0TT

First published 1989
© Gay Search and Geoff Hamilton 1989
Reprinted 1990 (twice)

ISBN 0 563 21501 1

Set in 10 on 12 Sabon
Printed and bound in Great Britain by
Butler & Tanner Ltd, Frome and London
Colour Separations by Technik Litho Plates Ltd,
Berkhamsted
Jacket/cover printed by Richard Clay Ltd, Norwich

CONTENTS

First time planting

In an ideal world all new gardeners would take over a plot that received sun all day and had lovely, fertile, easily worked soil that would grow anything they cared to plant in it. It's not an ideal world, though, and only a very few, very lucky gardeners take over such a plot. But the truly marvellous thing about gardening is that *anyone* who is prepared to learn just a few basic rules can do it successfully, regardless of the conditions, and the enormous pleasure and satisfaction to be got over the years from growing plants well is unlike almost anything else in this life – except perhaps seeing your children grow up, well and happy.

The basic rule for first time planting is: don't try to fight nature – work with it instead. You can't make a shady garden sunny, for instance, but you can choose to grow shade-loving plants that are every bit as beautiful as the sun lovers. And while of course there's plenty you can do to improve poor soil, you can't totally alter its character. A chalky soil, for instance, will never be a rich, acid loam.

Which Way Does the Garden Face?

You need to know, first of all, which way your garden faces, because that affects how much sun it gets and therefore which plants will thrive. If you get early-morning sun on the back of your house, and lose it after midday, your garden faces east. If you get sun only in the afternoon, it faces west. If, as you stand with your back to the house, the sun rises to the left of your garden, travels over the garden and sets on the right – lucky you: your garden faces south. If the sun rises to the right, though, and travels across the garden in the opposite direction, the garden faces north. In midsummer, when the sun is at its highest in the sky, a north-facing garden gets quite a lot of sunlight, but in spring, autumn and winter, when the sun is much lower in the sky, the garden will be largely in the shadow of your own and your neighbours' houses. While a north-

facing garden isn't ideal, there are so many superb plants that thrive in shade that if your garden didn't have any shade you would have to create some!

You need to look at surrounding features, too. Obviously, if there's a 20 m sycamore or even a 6 m factory wall at the bottom of your west-facing garden, you are not going to get much of the afternoon sun which, theoretically, you could expect.

Shade-lovers, like white bleeding heart (*Dicentra spectabilis* 'Alba'), ferns, hostas, euphorbias and the deep-rose-pink-flowered *Daphne retusa*, thrive in Beth Chatto's woodland garden in early summer.

The Answer Lies ...

It's also absolutely essential to know what sort of soil you have – whether it's clay, sand, chalk or medium loam, whether it is acid or alkaline (more of this later) – and to learn which plants will grow well in it. One of the real joys of gardening is that for every plant that won't thrive in your soil, there are others, just as beautiful, that will. If you have an alkaline limy soil, for example, like Rosemary Verey's at Barnsley House in Gloucestershire, you won't be able to grow rhododendrons or camellias, which need an acid soil, but you can grow shrubs like sweetly scented winter- and spring-flowering viburnums, lilac and mock orange (*Philadelphus*) as successfully as she does.

If you have a damp clay soil, alpines, which need thin, gravelly, free-draining soil, will simply rot away, but you could grow a wide range of colourful primulas, irises and astilbes, as well as many stunning foliage plants like hostas and rodgersias. Beth Chatto's bog garden at White Barns near Colchester, Essex, which we also visited for the television series 'First Time Planting', looks marvellous throughout the spring and summer and is a prime example of what can be achieved, with a bit of work, on the most unpromising, heavy, waterlogged soil.

The easiest and best way to start learning about your soil is to pick it up and handle it. If it feels sticky and you can mould it easily into a ball when it's wet, you have a heavy clay soil. If it feels silky between your fingers, you have a silt soil which has many of the same problems as clay and is treated in much the same way. If the soil feels very gritty and won't hold together in a ball no matter how hard you squeeze, it is sandy. If your soil looks dry, greyish and crumbly and contains a lot of stone, flints and even pieces of white chalk, that's what you're gardening on – chalk. Most soils, of course, are a mixture of these various extreme types, but even so it should be pretty obvious from the feel which mixture or 'loam' you have. If you have drawn first prize in the horticultural raffle of life, you will have a 'medium loam' – a rich, dark brown soil that retains moisture but is never waterlogged and is so fertile that you daren't stick your fingers in it for fear they'll grow roots!

The other absolutely essential fact you must know about your soil before you buy so much as a packet of seeds is its pH – whether it is acid or alkaline – because, without being too dramatic about it, the amount of lime in the soil is a matter of life or death for some plants. Rhododendrons, for example, are lime haters and on an alkaline soil they will simply die.

Adding water to a soil sample.

Checking the results of a soil test.

Soil-testing kits are available from all garden centres and are both cheap and easy to use. What you do is take a small sample of your soil and leave it to dry out. Then you place it in the test tube that comes with the kit, add the chemical provided and top up with distilled water. (Don't use tap water – its own pH varies from area to area and could affect your result.) Shake the test tube, then leave it to settle. Eventually the soil settles at the bottom of the tube and you are left with a coloured liquid on the top, which you then compare with the colours on the chart provided. Roughly speaking, the more orange the colour of the liquid, the lower the pH and the more acid your soil. Neutral soil, with a pH of 7, produces a mid-green liquid, while a dark green indicates an alkaline soil. If yours is a neutral-to-acid soil, you can grow most ornamental plants with ease. (If you wanted to grow vegetables in an acid soil, you would need to add lime to increase the alkalinity in all areas except the patch for potatoes, which are not averse to acid conditions.)

While it's relatively easy to make an acid soil more alkaline by adding lime, making an alkaline soil more acid could well have been one of the labours of Hercules! Adding lorry loads of peat will only have a temporary effect on chalky soil, so if you are absolutely desperate to grow camellias and rhododendrons, grow them in either raised beds or containers filled with peaty soil.

Once you know what sort of soil you are dealing with, even if you are lucky enough to have the rare and much prized 'medium loam', the next step is to start improving it.

CLAY

Clay is without doubt the most difficult soil initially, because when it's wet, it's a sticky, boggy morass, and when it's dry, it's as hard as concrete, and neither of these states is exactly hospitable to plants. That's the bad news. The good news is that, with a fair bit of hard work, a clay soil will grow far better plants than a very light, sandy soil ever can.

Those of you who saw our first television series, 'First Time Garden', will remember the appalling mud patch behind a brand-new house in Birmingham with which we started out, and the rather attractive, colourful, 'young' garden with trees, shrubs, perennials and annuals, as well as fruit and vegetables, with which we finished up some seven months later. What we took on was the garden that had everything – skip loads of rubble, barrow loads of red builders' sand, a 'hard pan' (a solid layer of soil compacted to a rock-like hardness by weeks of heavy plant moving backwards and forwards across it) and really thick, sticky clay soil that you could cut into slices with a spade and then make into passable pots!

The main problem with heavy clay soils (and with silt soils) is very bad drainage. In Beth Chatto's case a large area of her garden was actually spring-bearing land with a ditch running through it, so when she started work on it in 1960 it really was waterlogged. What she did was first of all dam the ditch to make a series of small ponds and improve the drainage of the rest by digging drainage ditches. If your soil is really heavy and wet, you may have to install a drainage system, but fortunately that's an extreme situation and you're unlikely to be that unlucky.

The best way to improve an averagely sticky clay or silt soil is to start by double-digging it (digging the soil to two spades' depth) and working in both coarse grit – about one barrow load to every 2 or 3 square metres – and organic matter well mixed through into all levels of the soil. The grit will open up the soil and allow air and water to pass more freely through it. The organic matter helps to open up the soil too, but in the case of well-made garden compost, or well-rotted animal manure, it also contains essential plant nutrients and provides a home for the millions of soil organisms that are vital to plant growth. When you've finished double-digging, spread a thick layer of organic matter over the area. It will soon get worked into the soil by the rain and the worms.

If you don't have any garden compost or a ready source of animal manure, you can use spent mushroom compost. It's a mixture of well-rotted horse manure and peat, but it also contains a small amount of lime. That's fine if your soil is already limy or if you want to use it on the vegetable patch, but not if you have an acid soil and want to grow acid-loving plants. It doesn't contain many plant nutrients by the time you get it, either, so you will have to add those in the form of fertilisers.

Alternatively, use pure peat. This contains no plant nutrients at all, and it is one of the most expensive soil conditioners there is, but it does do the job extremely well, so if you can't lay your hands on anything else, use it as a last resort.

By adding all this organic matter and grit to the soil you are raising your borders above the level of your lawn, which will also help them to drain more freely.

When you dig heavy clay, you need to get your timing just right. In the early stages, before you've 'tamed' it with organic matter, you'll have to catch it between the times when it is dry and hard as a rock and the times when it has become thoroughly waterlogged and you're knee-deep in mud. The best way is to dig it over roughly in the autumn – ideally when it's drying out but still moist – and leave it for the winter frosts to work on. As it dries out it cracks, and when water gets into those cracks and freezes it forces them wider apart, breaking the soil down into smaller and smaller clods. With a bit of luck and few good hard frosts, you will find that in the spring you need only rake it down.

Incidentally, you should *never* walk on heavy soil when it is wet, since you are simply compounding the problems it suffers. If for some reason you simply have to walk on the soil, you should always put down wide scaffolding planks to spread your weight.

Planting as much as you possibly can also helps heavy soil, because the plants' roots open it up as they grow, and even after the plants have been removed, in the case of annuals, or indeed vegetable crops, the remaining roots still perform that service. So if you can, aim to keep the soil covered with plants all the time.

SAND

On first acquaintance, and compared to heavy clay soils, sandy soils are a doddle to cultivate. Free-draining, they are workable when other types of soil are still waterlogged, they warm up quickly in spring which is ideal for raising early crops, and they are very easy to dig over in preparation for planting. But every Eden has its serpent, and in the case of sandy soils it's the fact that they dry out very quickly, losing not only moisture but valuable plant nutrients too. For that reason they demand large amounts of organic matter which help retain moisture in the soil, and plant nutrients in the form of fertilisers every year. However, since organic matter will work its way through the thin topsoil very quickly and into the subsoil, it is a waste of time – and compost – to dig it in too deeply. Either dig it into the top few centimetres of soil only or simply spread it over the surface and allow the elements and the worms to work it in for you. Applying organic matter this way – as a mulch – has another advantage. Because sandy soils lose moisture through surface evaporation as well as through free drainage, covering the surface with a mulch helps to prevent that happening.

One section of Beth Chatto's garden is poor, thin, gravelly soil, so what she did was to improve it by adding large amounts of organic matter, and then choose only plants that would thrive in near-drought conditions – many of them from the Mediterranean – for once the borders are planted and mulched with a thick layer of compost or manure, they are never watered.

CHALK

Chalky soils have many of the same advantages and problems as sand – they are very free-draining and are rarely too wet to work, but they lose water and nutrients very rapidly. They have an additional problem in that the layer of topsoil is usually shallow and chalky soils are always very alkaline, which limits the range of plants that will grow happily in them. The way to improve a chalky soil is much the same as with sand – add lots of organic matter and fertiliser, and keep the surface of the soil covered as far as possible to prevent evaporation. If you can use organic matter that is acidic, like peat, well-rotted manure, garden compost or grass cuttings, for digging in and mulching, you will help, though only in a small way, to counteract the alkalinity of the soil. Rosemary Verey, whose beautiful garden is on very alkaline Cotswold limestone, double-dug her soil when she originally made the borders and added lots of manure. Every autumn the beds are mulched with leaf mould. 'We do have masses of leaves here, but they take a whole year to rot down, provided they are kept moist,' she said. 'If they're dry when they're collected up, we have to water the heap. If we find we're running out, we mix the remaining leaf mould with peat and a slow-release fertiliser like bone meal. I do try to avoid using manure if I can because of the weed seeds it usually contains.'

MEDIUM LOAM

If you are lucky enough to have medium loam, even though it won't need lots of work to improve it, it will still benefit from an annual dose of manure or compost. Soil is like life – what you get out of it depends to a large extent on what you put into it.

Planting Techniques

TREES

When all trees were sold bare-rooted, gardeners really had no choice but to plant either in autumn or in early spring. The autumn was considered the best time by many because the trees had a chance to get established before the winter frosts and so were well placed to take off in spring. The soil is still warm, for one thing, there is unlikely to be a prolonged dry spell and, once their leaves have fallen, most plants put their energies into a final spurt of root growth before closing down, as it were, for the winter. The only disadvantage of autumn planting is that a prolonged spell of really cold winter weather can kill off a few less hardy plants while they are still not properly established, though that applies more to shrubs and herbaceous perennials than to trees.

If you are planting bare-rooted trees, the old rules still apply, though you can plant any time up to March when the ground isn't either waterlogged or frozen. If you buy container-grown trees, obviously you can plant at any time of year, though again it's easier in the autumn when drought is unlikely and you don't need to be quite so careful about frequent watering.

Use a cane or a spade to check that the top of the rootball is level with the soil.

How to plant container-grown trees

By the time you've got round to buying your trees, you will have already prepared your borders by digging over the soil and improving it in whichever ways are necessary (see pages 10–12). It can't be stressed too strongly that you must never simply dig a hole in uncultivated ground, throw in a bit of peat and plant your tree in it. If you do that on a clay soil, the hole will act as a sump, drawing water from the land around, so that you're planting your tree in cold, waterlogged soil. If you're lucky, the tree will just be very slow to start into growth; if you're not, the roots will either be deprived of air and so drown, or will rot away, and the tree will die.

Before you actually start digging your hole, give the rootball of the tree, still in its container, a thorough soaking. Not only will this make it easier to remove the pot when the time comes, but it will also ensure that the roots and the soil around them are really moist before you plant them, something that's much harder to do once they're in the ground.

Dig a hole slightly bigger than the container. Check that it is deep enough by putting the container in the hole, then laying a bamboo cane, or even your spade, across it. If the cane rests on the soil on both sides *and* the top of the container touches it, the hole is deep enough.

If your soil is low on organic matter, add a few spadefuls of peat and a couple of handfuls of blood, fish and bone meal to the pile of soil you've dug out. Then remove the tree carefully from its pot. If it's a thin, black polythene one, slice it off with a sharp knife. If it's a rigid, plastic pot and you've watered it thoroughly beforehand, the tree plus rootball should lift out fairly easily. Should it stick in its pot, try holding the trunk of the tree and twisting it very gently or try gently squeezing the sides of the pot just to loosen the soil. If all else fails, you'll have to cut the pot away using a Stanley knife or something similar. Put the rootball into the hole and make sure that the tree is facing the right way. Many trees have a pretty obvious front if you look at the shape, so make sure that's

Right: When you start to fill in the hole, give the plant's roots some good topsoil from around the edge. Replace it with some of the surplus you have dug out.

Far right: Nailing the tree tie to the stake keeps it firmly in place.

Use another hammer held firmly against the back of the stake to keep it rigid while you hammer in the nail.

facing the point from which you'll be looking at it most often. Then start carefully shovelling in the soil. When you've filled the hole, firm the soil with the ball of your foot. The aim is to get rid of any large air pockets but not to compress the soil too tightly together, so go gently.

It's a very good idea to use the surplus soil to build a small retaining wall around the tree about 30 cm (1 ft) out from the trunk. When you give the newly planted tree a thorough soaking, that wall will help keep the water where you want it – directly over the rootball.

Staking

Almost all new trees need staking, but recent research has shown that short stakes – reaching only one third of the way up the trunk – are more efficient than the traditional, much longer ones. Allowing the top of the tree to sway about in the wind, it seems, thickens the base of the trunk and helps strengthen the root system.

You'll need two stakes of 5 × 5 cm (2 × 2 in) timber. To work out the length, measure the tree's trunk and divide by three (to give on third of its length) and add 45 cm (18 in) to hammer into the ground. Hammer the stakes in just outside the rootball on either side, then nail a cross-piece between them. Attach it to the trunk with a special plastic tree tie which has a collar to prevent it chafing. Whatever you do, don't use wire or nylon twine which will cut into the tree as it grows and either kill it or allow diseases in.

Alternatively, you can use just one stake, the same length as described above, and hammer it diagonally into the ground behind the tree and close to the trunk. Then use a tree tie in the same way.

Planting evergreens

Evergreens, like conifers, are best planted in September or left until April or even May. They are almost always supplied either in containers (in which case plant them as you would any container-grown tree) or 'rootballed' – that is, they have been dug up with a good ball of soil around the roots, which is then wrapped in sacking for delivery. Leave the sacking round the roots until the moment you are ready to plant – it not only protects them from damage but also stops the soil washing away from the roots when you water the tree, which you will need to do plentifully and often. When you have dug the correct-sized hole, place the rootball, sacking and all, in it and cut away as much of the sacking as you can easily reach. What's left underneath the rootball will soon rot away in the soil. Then finish planting in the same way as before.

Planting bare-rooted trees

The key to success with bare-rooted trees is to make sure that the roots never dry out. The very small roots which take up essential nutrients, as well as water, will die if they're exposed to the sun or to drying winds for any length of time. This means that if the trees arrive at a time when you can't plant them right away, you must 'heel them in'. Dig a trench of about a spade's depth, throwing the soil forward. Lay the trees in the trench with the roots at the bottom and the trunk leaning away from you, on to the soil you've thrown forward. Then cover the roots by digging another trench behind the first and throwing the soil forward on to them. When you're ready to plant, remove the trees to where you're going to plant them but keep the roots covered with wet sacking or an old wet towel. Dig a hole wide enough to take the roots when they are spread out and deep enough for the soil, once the tree's planted, to be exactly level with the soil-mark on the trunk of the tree, which indicates the level at which it was grown in the nursery. Check this using a bamboo cane or a spade placed across the hole. Now take a stake one third the length of the trunk, plus 45 cm (18 in), and hammer it well into the hole.

Before you plant check the roots, and if any are broken or damaged cut them back cleanly with a sharp knife or secateurs. Place the tree in the hole, arranging the roots around the stake if need be, and then put in a little fine soil (mixed with peat and blood, fish and bone meal) over the roots. Hold the trunk of the tree firmly and jerk it up and down a few times, so that the soil settles in between the roots. Half-fill the hole and tread it firmly but gently with the ball of your foot. The aim, again, is to eliminate large air pockets in which the roots would dry out and die, but to avoid compressing the soil too much. Refill the hole completely and firm the soil with your foot. Attach the trunk to the stake with a special tree tie, and mulch around the trunk with well-rotted compost or manure.

Caring for newly planted trees

Whether they're container-grown or bare-rooted, it is *absolutely essential* to keep newly planted trees well watered. It's a sad fact that over half of all trees and shrubs planted die within the first year, and there's no doubt that failure to give them enough water is the primary reason. And that doesn't mean the odd bucketful or standing there for five minutes with the hose. It takes some time for soil to be saturated at the lower levels where the roots are, and if you only wet the surface, thirsty roots will come looking for water there and will be even more susceptible to damage from hot sun or drying winds. So once your tree is planted, put the hose (running a bit faster than a trickle but not full on) on the rootball and leave it for half an hour or so. If you've built a retaining wall of soil as described on page 14, obviously that will help keep the water where it's most needed. In warm weather check regularly that the soil is moist a few centimetres below the surface. If it is not, water again. And don't think if there's been a light shower that you needn't bother. Unless the heavens have opened for an hour or two, you'll still need to do it!

Evergreens need special care when it comes to watering. All trees lose water through their leaves, and since evergreens retain theirs all year, they are losing water through them constantly. Unless you replace it, therefore, the leaves will start to shrivel and turn brown. For the same reason it's essential to protect from frost evergreens that you haven't got round to planting yet. In a plastic pot the rootball can freeze very easily, and with the water turned to ice the tree can't take it up and suffers effectively from drought.

To protect it dig the container into the soil or, if that's not possible, heap something like peat or bark around the pot.

CLIMBERS

The most important thing to remember when it comes to planting climbers is that the soil at the bottom of a fence or wall (and particularly a house wall where the overhanging eaves keep most of the rain off it) is very dry. So always add lots of organic matter to the planting hole and make sure that the climber itself is at least 30 cm (1 ft) away from the wall.

As for support, whether or not it's necessary depends on the type of climber. There are three main groups, the first of which encompasses the self-clingers like ivy, Virginia creeper and the climbing hydrangea. Initially, when they've just been planted, they'll need some help to get a grip, but tying the young stem to a bamboo cane which slopes up against the wall or fence is usually all that is necessary.

The second group, climbers and twiners, like honeysuckle, jasmine and clematis, which attach themselves by twining either their stems or their leaf stalks around something else, do need support. There are a number of alternatives.

The cheapest method for fences is to stretch horizontal wires between the fence posts, starting about 60 cm (2 ft) from the ground.

Fixing trellis to a fence as a support for climbers.

Place them about 30 cm (1 ft) apart and secure them with staples. To make a mesh you then weave lengths of thinner wire vertically through these 30 cm (1 ft) apart, and secure them on the top and bottom horizontal wires.

To make a support system on a wall you can fix wooden battens 25×35 mm ($1 \times 1\frac{1}{2}$ in) to the wall first with Rawlplugs and screws, and then attach wires to them as described in the preceding paragraph. This lifts the wires clear of the wall, not only allowing twiners to get behind them, but also allowing air to circulate and help prevent diseases like mildew on roses. Alternatively, you can, of course, use wooden or plastic trellising, fixed to the fence posts or the battens, but it's more expensive and, in the case of the plastic stuff, more obtrusive than the wires.

Climbers in the third group, which includes roses and wall shrubs like Moroccan broom (*Cytisus battandieri*), have no means of support, visible or otherwise, and so they do need to be tied. You could use a framework of wires or trellis, or you could try Rosemary Verey's method. To support a large beauty bush (*Kolkwitzia amabilis*), for example, she has fixed a piece of chicken wire about 2×2 m (6×6 ft) to the wall with special lead-headed wall nails, and has tied the stems to it. From only a few feet away, the wire is invisible. You could use chicken wire for twining plants, but it would have to be fixed to battens, not attached directly to the wall, because there would be no space for the plant to grow through and behind the wire otherwise. Lead-headed nails have pliable flanges of metal on the top, which can be bent around wires or plant stems. These nails can also be very useful for fixing climbers that need support in only a few places (some climbing roses, for example) directly onto a wall, but if you find you're having to bang in more and more of them, one of the other methods is preferable.

SHRUBS

Shrubs are planted in exactly the same way as you'd plant trees, though very few shrubs, apart from roses and some hedging plants, are sold bare-rooted these days. And, of course, shrubs don't need staking.

HERBACEOUS PLANTS

The principles of planting herbaceous plants are really much the same as for trees, shrubs and climbers: prepare the ground well, give the plants a really thorough soaking in their pots a few hours before you plant them and add a handful or two of rose fertiliser or a general-purpose fertiliser like Growmore to the planting hole.

Since you'll have made a planting plan (and you will have made one, won't you? See Chapter Two), you should know exactly what goes where, so place the plants, still in their pots, on the soil to see how they look. If they don't look right, it's easy to try some other

grouping at this stage. In fact, most herbaceous plants are very easy-going even if you realise, after you've planted them, that they're in the wrong place. Provided that you give them a good soak before you dig them up and another afterwards, and keep them well watered until they've settled in, you can even move them in full flower: after looking a bit floppy for a day or two, they'll perk up again. Obviously, it's better if you don't have to do that, though.

Above: Building a small retaining wall of soil around newly planted shrubs or trees helps keep the water where it is most needed – directly above the rootball.

Above left: Give climbers a good start on a chicken wire support by weaving the young growths, or leaf stalks, in and out.

Before planting, check that the rootball will come out of the pot. If it won't, hold the plant firmly at its base, turn the pot upside down and tap its bottom.

If your soil wasn't too bad to start with and you've prepared it really well, you should be able, with a trowel, to make a hole just large enough to take the rootball, and firm it in. Beth Chatto is a great believer in digging a large hole – what that great Edwardian gardener Gertrude Jekyll used to call 'a five pound hole for a sixpenny plant' – and filling it with organic matter before she plants her perennials. If you still have heavy clay or thin, sandy soil despite your best efforts, it's worth a try. Once your plants are in, firm the soil around them with your knuckles (but without compressing it too much) and then give them a thorough watering.

ANNUALS

Half-hardy annuals which you've bought from the garden centre should never be planted out until all danger of frost is past – which means the end of May for the South, early June for the Midlands, and even mid-June for the North and Scotland. It is tempting, if there is a spell of nice weather in early May, to rush off and buy your half-hardy annuals and get them in. Some years you'll get away with it, but in other years one severe, late frost can kill the lot.

Prepare the top few centimetres of soil before you plant, adding a little organic matter and some general-purpose or rose fertiliser, resisting the temptation to be too generous or you'll wind up with lots of lush leafy growth and not many flowers. Soak the plants well beforehand, and then remove them carefully from their trays. If they're in individual cells, simply plant as they are. If they're in one tray, remove the whole block and gently tear the plants apart or even cut them with a sharp knife if necessary. Although the object of using annuals, in part anyway, is to fill the gaps while shrubs and herbaceous plants are slowly growing, be careful not to plant them too close to the permanent subjects. If you do, they'll be competing with them for nutrients, moisture and light, which will slow down their rate of growth.

Hardy annuals are sown directly into the soil where you want them to flower, and you can start sowing as soon as the soil is dry enough to cultivate – in March or early April in a good year. If you have a heavy soil, it's well worth covering the area you plan to sow with annuals with a piece of clear polythene in the previous autumn. This not only prevents the soil from getting saturated by winter rains, but it also helps it to warm up earlier in spring.

In mixed borders annuals look best in informal clumps or drifts, so scratch out a shape, free-hand, on the soil with a stick. Within that shape, it's a good idea to sow the seeds in straight lines about 15–20 cm (6–8 ins) apart, rather than to scatter them broadcast. Weed seeds germinate at the same time as the annuals, but if you've sown your seeds in straight lines, it's very easy to see which are weeds and which are not. Once they're thinned out and growing well, you're not aware of the straight lines at all.

Incidentally, if you have heavy clay soil, try making your seed drills a good bit wider and deeper than normal and filling them with fine seed compost. That is a far more hospitable environment for delicate, emerging roots than thick, wet clay. By the time the roots of the young plants have outgrown the drill, they are tough enough to cope with the clay.

After sowing your seeds, cover them lightly with soil (or seed compost in the case of heavy clay) by running a rake between the drills. Then tap the soil down gently with the back of the rake. Once the seedlings emerge, keep them free of weeds and, when they're big enough to handle, thin them out to 15–20 cm (6–8 in) apart by removing all the seedlings in between. It is very hard for first time gardeners to pull up and discard perfectly healthy seedlings that they've grown, but it's essential. If you don't thin them out enough, you'll wind up with spindly, rather sickly plants.

You can start a few hardy annuals in small peat pots or poly-styrene cells on a sunny windowsill in March, which means that when you plant them out in May they'll have a head start on the weeds. Sow them in moist seed compost – two to a pot or cell if they're large seeds like lavatera or a small pinch sown centrally if they're smaller – then cover them to their own depth with seed compost or vermiculite (which you can buy from the garden centre). Cover the pots or trays with opaque polythene (those white bags they give you in supermarkets for frozen food are ideal) and put them in the airing cupboard, having first checked that it's not too hot for the variety you're sowing. Check the seed every day and when the first one germinates take the pot or tray out and stand it on a light windowsill. With large seeds, if both germinate, remove the weaker seedling. Where you've sown a small pinch of seed, leave the clump to grow and plant it out eventually as it is.

In a greenhouse you get light from all directions, but on a windowsill you get it from only one and so your seedlings will grow towards it, making them thin and spindly. You can help stop this by turning them regularly or, better still, making them a 'Barnsdale light box' – any good-sized cardboard box with the top and front removed and the remaining sides, back and bottom covered with aluminium foil. That will reflect the light around the seedlings and encourage sturdier, more even growth.

Gradually harden off your seedlings by putting the pots or trays outside on dry, mild days, at first bringing them in again at night. Plant them out in May at the recommended planting distance for the variety.

Lavatera trimestris 'Mont Blanc': just one packet of seeds sown in a large drift makes a stunning display.

In late spring the dying foliage of these bulbs will be hidden by the emerging growth of the hardy perennials planted in a rough triangle around them.

BULBS

Spring-flowering bulbs, which really are nature's reward for getting through the long, grey winter, should be planted from August onwards, though tulips shouldn't be planted until November in case they start into growth too quickly and are nobbled by the frost. Summer-flowering bulbs, like summer hyacinth, should be planted in spring because many of them are tender and that way the growth doesn't emerge until all danger of frost is past. Lilies can be planted in either autumn or spring.

The one thing all bulbs hate is waterlogged soil – it rots them in no time – so if you have a heavy soil, always plant them on a thick layer of coarse grit. They're also not very keen on being planted too shallowly for that means in summer they're likely to get too hot and to be starved of moisture. A quick rule of thumb for bulbs is to plant them at three times their own depth at least, so that they wind up with twice their own depth of soil on top of them. A bulb that's 2.5 cm (1 in) deep, for example, needs to be planted in a hole at least 7.5 cm (3 in) deep so that it has 5 cm (2 in) of soil on top of it.

You can plant large bulbs, like tulips or daffodils, individually using a bulb planter (get one with a soil-releasing mechanism other-wise you can spend ages trying to remove the plug of soil from the planter!) Alternatively, you can plant them in a group in one large hole. That's certainly the best method for small bulbs. Again, in a mixed border, clumps or drifts of bulbs are much better than straight lines or singletons dotted about the place, and *en masse* they make much more of an impact too. You often read that the way to achieve a natural effect with bulbs is to throw a handful in the air and plant them where they land. That's fine if you've got lots of space and you're lucky – all too often what seems to happen is that 99 per cent of them fall in a huddle together, while the remaining 1 per cent land a foot away. It is easier to draw an irregular shape on the soil with a stick – a rough kidney shape, for example – dig it out to the required depth and then place the individual bulbs pretty evenly within it.

If your bulbs are to remain permanently in your borders (and few people have the inclination to lift, dry and store them – or the space in a small garden), you need to plant them where they're unlikely to be disturbed. It's so easy, once all trace of them has disappeared in summer, to slice through them with the spade as you merrily dig away. One answer is to plant them around shrubs where you're unlikely to be digging anyway.

Another answer, and one that also solves the major problem of what to do with the bulbs' dying foliage in those six weeks or so between the end of flowering and the time when you can safely remove it with no harm to next year's flowers, is to plant them with your perennials. If you're going to plant three cranesbills –

Planting these red tulips in one large clump makes a far greater impact than dotting them around.

Geranium 'Johnson's Blue', for instance – in an irregular triangle shape, fill the centre of that triangle with small bulbs like crocuses or squills. In winter and spring, when the bulbs are growing and in flower, all you can see of the cranesbills are small brown tufts. By the time the bulbs have finished flowering, the cranesbills have started into growth, and by the time the bulbs' foliage is beginning to die off, the cranesbills' new fresh green leaves will hide it completely. Another good combination, for the same reason, is tulips or dwarf daffodils planted with day lilies (*Hemerocallis*) or crocosmia. In addition, the fact that they all have similar, strap-like leaves means that the foliage of the former blends in perfectly with the new growth of the latter,

It's all too easy to forget about feeding bulbs – out of sight, out of mind – but a handful or two of blood, fish and bone, or a watering with a liquid plant food such as Phostrogen, once flowering is over will pay dividends with next year's flowers.

CHAPTER TWO

Designing your borders

Although there is a certain very real satisfaction in laying patios and lawns, in building walls and even in double-digging grotty soil to make the borders, there's no doubt that the real fun in gardening is the planting. Having built your easel, as it were, and having prepared your canvas, you are ready to start thinking about painting the picture. The most important phrase here is 'thinking about', for the key to successful planting lies in planning. Simply running off to the garden centre, cheque book at the ready, and filling up the car with the first things that take your eye is almost certainly a recipe for disaster. Apart from anything else, what catches your eye is most likely to be what's currently in flower, so you could end up with a garden full of colour for three weeks at that particular time, and then no colour for the rest of the year.

A patch of burnt orange alstroemeria brightens up the mainly blue, white and mauve planting in this sunny, south-facing border at Barnsley House.

By now you will know what sort of soil you have and how much – or how little – sun your borders are going to get. What you need to know next is which plants are going to thrive in the conditions you are offering, and we'll be giving you lists for north-, south-, east- and west-facing borders suitable for different soil types later on in the book. A good, well-illustrated plant encyclopaedia will provide you with some idea of what the various plants look like and will give you other useful information about their size (height and spread) and their habit (whether they're upright or bushy or spreading), but there is no substitute for seeing the real thing. Of course, you can see plants at the garden centre, but a two-year-old *Clematis montana* in a 20 cm (8 in) pot gives you no clue to the fact that it will grow up to 12 m (40 ft) in four or five years and smother everything – animal, vegetable or mineral – in its path!

The best way to learn about plants is to see them growing in other people's gardens. Not only will you discover how mature plants look in a real garden setting, but you'll also observe how they work in relation to the other plants around them in terms of size, shape, flower colour and also shape and colour of foliage. No plant – in a border, anyway – is an island, and how it fits in with the rest of the plants you choose is just as important as its own individual qualities. Certainly the key to creating attractive borders lies in choosing plants that are pleasing in their own right but which also bring out the best in their neighbours.

For instance, in the first time garden featured in the television programme of the same name, we planted the climbing hydrangea (*Hydrangea petiolaris*) on the fence behind the small ornamental crab apple (*Malus* 'Profusion') because the former's new, fresh green leaves in spring make a splendid backdrop for the latter's coppery new foliage, and its flat heads of small, white flowers take over once the ornamental crab's purple-red flowers have first faded to pink and then fallen.

There are many famous gardens open to the public which are well worth visiting, and it's advisable always to go armed with notebook and pencil and, ideally, a camera. You will see some superb plants and some extremely imaginative planting that way, but many first time gardeners may find the sort of herbaceous borders 30 m (100 ft) long and 3 or 4 m (10 or 12 ft) wide that are features in many of these gardens more off-putting than helpful because the scale seems far too large to adapt to the small patch that most of us have these days. However, don't be put off: look at small sections of those grand borders and note which plants look good with each other. The great bonus of many of these large gardens is that the plants are labelled.

It's also a very good idea to visit some of the many small, private gardens up and down the country, opened to the public in aid of various charities once or twice a year. They are listed, region by region, in either of the 'Yellow Books' – officially *Gardens in England and Wales Open to the Public*, available from garden centres or bookshops at £1.50, and *Scotland's Gardens*, also £1.50. That way you can see gardens created by amateurs, faced with situations similar to your own. Quite soon you'll start to get a feel for the sort of planting you like best and the sort of colour schemes you prefer.

The style of planting you decide on is very much a matter of personal taste, and if you want a garden full of hybrid tea roses, there is absolutely nothing to stop you. But for most first time gardeners the cottage garden principle is probably the easiest and the best. That doesn't mean growing only traditional cottage garden plants; it's more adopting the same style of mixed planting, with trees, shrubs, herbaceous plants, annuals, bulbs, herbs, fruit and even vegetables, all growing together in the same beds. It's the principle we used in the first time garden, in which trees like mountain ash (*Sorbus aucuparia*), shrubs like Mexican orange blossom (*Choisya ternata*), herbaceous plants like lupins and hostas, and annuals like busy Lizzie (*Impatiens*), shared the beds perfectly happily with apple trees, tomato plants, dwarf French beans and lettuces.

Practically any type of plant can be grown in mixed borders, though some varieties are more suitable than others. Take roses. Hybrid tea and floribunda rose bushes are deservedly the most popular and widely grown for their large flowers and striking colours, but many of them are too stiff in their growth for mixed borders. A better choice, perhaps, would be the less formal, small shrub or patio roses like 'The Fairy', which has masses of small, rose-pink flowers from July to the first hard frosts, as well as very attractive, small, glossy green leaves; it makes a spreading bush about 60 cm (2 ft) high and 1 m (3 ft) across. Another good choice would be the slightly smaller 'Bianco', which has large clusters of creamy white flowers, or the pretty, pale pink 'Bonica'.

Colour Schemes

As you look at different gardens, you will soon begin to find out which colours you prefer. Perhaps you like a riot of strong, 'hot' colours – reds, golds, oranges, purples – or perhaps you prefer something quieter, with pinks, mauves, soft blues and whites. It's worth remembering that a garden isn't like a room where all four sides are expected to be decorated in much the same way. There's no reason why each of your borders shouldn't have a different colour scheme, nor indeed any reason why the colour schemes shouldn't differ according to the season – perhaps blue, white and yellow in the spring; blues, pinks, mauves and whites in summer; and warm reds, gold and oranges in autumn.

Choosing colours carefully is very important in a small garden. Too many different ones dotted about in the same border either look a mess – giving a 'dolly mixture' effect – or simply cancel each other out. That's not to say that you can't have reds, yellows, blues, pinks, mauves and whites together in the same border: you can, provided you use at least some of those colours in largish blocks and plant in such a way that each group complements rather than clashes with (or, 'swears at', as old gardeners say) its neighbour. If you look at the colour wheel on page 28 you can see that colours next to each other – red and yellow, for example – blend very well, while those opposite each other – red and blue – contrast. Which you prefer is, of course, a matter of taste.

Where you place colours in the garden is important too. Strong colours draw the eye, so they are probably best planted closest to the house; if planted at the end of a border, they have the effect of foreshortening it and making the garden look smaller. Pale colours have the opposite effect: planted at the far end of the garden, they can make it look bigger.

Pale colours – white, cream and very soft yellow particularly – can also be used to 'cool down' hot colours that would otherwise clash, like acid yellow and rich purple. They can also be used to weave a border together, planted at irregular intervals throughout it. In one lovely cottage garden in Oxfordshire pale blue and white bellflowers (*Campanula persicifolia*) had seeded themselves at various points throughout the multi-coloured border, giving it unity and, as its owner said, making it look like fairyland.

It's interesting to note that the colours of many of our native flowers are rather soft and pale, which suits our soft light, while many of the really strong, vibrantly coloured flowers originate in hotter, sunnier climates than our own – the Mediterranean, South America, Africa – where the light is much clearer and harder.

Certainly bright colours look best in sunshine, so they are best placed in the sunniest border. Pale colours, which can look a bit washed out in bright sunlight, come into their own in soft light in the morning, in the evening and in shadow – a patch of white or very pale pink busy Lizzies (*Impatiens*) in a shady border really does gleam.

Single-colour borders or gardens – inspired by the famous White Garden at Sissinghurst in Kent – have become rather fashionable, but they are extremely difficult to do well, as even a gifted gardener like Rosemary Verey discovered.

'At first I tried to be terribly clever,' she said, 'and had a red border and a blue border and a yellow border, but they never actually worked. The most successful, and the only one I've kept, is the golden border, which has quite a lot of golden foliage – a golden elm (*Ulmus sarniensis* 'Dicksonii'), a honey locust (*Gleditsia triacanthos* 'Sunburst'), a golden privet (*Ligustrum ovalifolium*

Centre: The orange-reds of the spurge (*Euphorbia griffithii* 'Dixter') and *Geum* 'Borisii' blend well with the pale yellow of the irises, which also softens what would have been a stark contrast between the orange-reds and the purple flowers of the bugle (*Ajuga reptans* 'Atropurpurea')

Right: Once the candelabra primulas have finished flowering, the contrasts in form and colour of the surrounding foliage provide plenty of interest for the rest of the season.

'Aureum'), *Spiraea* × *bumalda* 'Goldflame' and a holly (*Ilex alter-clarensis* 'Lawsoniana'). There are some yellow flowers too, like the early-flowering rose, *Rosa cantabrigiensis*, and some yellow tulips, but most of the flowers are white – tulips again, Japanese anemones, the summer hyacinth (*Galtonia candicans*) and a white honesty with variegated leaves (*Lunaria biennis variegata* 'Alba'). In any single colour scheme I think it's very important to have just a splash of another colour, something unexpected, so in the middle of the golden border there is one large patch of the blue-flowered Jacob's ladder (*Polemonium caeruleum*).'

What can look very effective, though, is a border or part of a border planted in different tones that contain just a hint of the same primary colour. Take yellow, for instance: if you start with creamy white at one end of the spectrum and move through pale yellows, soft golds and oranges to warm, peachy pinks, you certainly haven't got a 'yellow' border. There is quite a lot of contrast, but at the same time the overall effect is mellow and pleasing.

FOLIAGE

The one colour which so often gets left out of discussions on the subject of garden colour schemes, and which is actually pre-dominant in any garden, is green. Not only is there the lawn which sets off the borders, but there is foliage too, and to talk about the 'forty shades of green' is probably an underestimate. There are very pale greens, dark greens, acid greens, lime greens, sage greens, matt greens, glossy greens; and greens variegated with white, with cream, with yellow, with gold, even with pink and purple. And of course not all foliage is green – there are many plants with grey leaves, everything from an almost-white silver to a deep, steely blue-grey; there are plants with golden leaves, with pink leaves, red, maroon, deep purple ... as you can see, it's perfectly possible to have a colourful garden without a single flower.

Foliage also offers a huge variety of shapes and sizes – from minute leaves, scarcely bigger than a pin head, like those of Corsican mint (*Mentha requienii*), to huge ones almost a metre across, like those of ornamental rhubarb (*Rheum palmatum*). There are very long, thin leaves, fat, round leaves, smooth ones, jagged ones, feathery ones, shiny ones, leathery ones, deeply veined ones ... the possibilities for choosing plants that will set each other off to perfection are almost endless. Not only do you have different colours to choose from, you have different shapes too. Just imagine how attractive the fine stems of Bowles' golden grass (*Milium effusum* 'Aureum') would look planted in a shady spot with a large, plain green, round-leafed hosta like 'Royal Standard'.

One of the main advantages that foliage has to offer any gardener is its long season of interest – far longer than any flowering plant will provide. Evergreens provide colour all year round, while deciduous trees and shrubs and herbaceous plants are attractive to look at for up to eight months. They may be particularly attractive in spring, when the new foliage first appears, and again in autumn when it turns red or gold.

Of course, all plants that flower have foliage too, so it's well worth taking that into account when you're making a choice. If you want to plant a weigela for its very pretty pink flowers in early summer, then instead of choosing one with plain green leaves why not opt for the variegated variety, *Weigela florida* 'Variegata', the pale green and cream foliage of which goes on looking attractive long after the flowers have faded?

Beth Chatto is a great believer in the virtues of foliage. 'For me, foliage plants are the comfortable furniture of the garden, the armchairs, the carpets and curtains,' she said. 'They provide a continuing pattern for a greater part of the year with their contrasting size, shape, texture, colour and form. Flowers are the lamps and the ornaments that add a bit of sparkle for a while!'

One of her borders in damp, heavy soil is a case in point. In spring and early summer the red and pink candelabra primulas are very attractive – 'the stars', she calls them – but once they've finished flowering, the foliage plants around them, 'the supporting cast' – the different willows, like silvery *Salix argentea* and the woolly willow, *Salix lanata*, the ornamental grasses and reeds – are equally attractive in their own right for the rest of the season.

There is a school of thought which maintains that large plants have no place in small gardens. While obviously it would be absurd to plant a weeping willow or one of the larger-growing rhododendrons where space is at a premium, some of the larger herbaceous plants can be very effective. One of the problems of newly planted gardens is that, inevitably, the trees and shrubs are relatively small, so it is difficult to get height into the borders in the first couple of years. Of course, you could buy much larger, more mature specimens; however, they not only cost a fortune but are also more difficult to get established and growing well. And once they are growing, you may find that within a couple of years they are too large for your border, so you'll either have to prune them back or get rid of them altogether. A much better – and cheaper – way of providing height is to choose one or two herbaceous plants which grow pretty large even in their first season – ornamental rhubarb (*Rheum palmatum*), for example, or one of the tall variegated grasses, like *Miscanthus sinensis* 'Variegatus' – but which, since they die down again every winter, are unlikely to outgrow their allotted space in your border.

When it comes to choosing foliage plants, scale is very important. While you can grow plants with very small leaves and plants with very large leaves in the same bed, they need to be separated by other plants with medium-sized leaves or they look rather strange.

Whatever the scale of the planting, though, Beth Chatto is a great believer in what she calls 'stop' plants: plants with large, relatively simple leaves to give the eye and the brain a rest, to act at the end of a border or part of a border in the same way as a full stop at the end of a sentence. In a border of comparatively small plants something like elephant's ears (*Bergenia*) or one of the plain hostas will serve this purpose very well, while in groups of larger plants ornamental rhubarb (*Rheum palmatum*) or even an evergreen shrub like the false castor-oil plant (*Fatsia japonica*, often thought of as a houseplant but actually very hardy) will do the trick.

It's also worth thinking about the overall shape of the plants you're thinking of growing, too, whether they're chosen for flowers or foliage. A border full of small, rounded hummocks, say, would look pretty dull. Although Rosemary Verey doesn't like colours that contrast – preferring those that blend – she is very keen on shapes that do. 'In one border, for instance, I have the lovely dwarf hebe (*Hebe rakaiensis*),' she explained, 'which forms a marvellous rounded mound of pale green foliage. With that I like to grow the evening primrose (*Oenothera biennis*) and the peach-leaved bellflower (*Campanula persicifolia*) which are both tall and spiky.'

Groups or Individuals?

In a small garden, when it comes to planting trees and larger shrubs, there usually isn't space to include more than one individual specimen, so the question of whether or not to plant in groups doesn't arise. When it comes to smaller shrubs and herbaceous plants, planting just one of each variety can result in the 'dolly mixture' effect mentioned earlier, in which some of the plants just get lost.

Beth Chatto is a firm believer in planting in groups – always odd numbers of plants, never even – which will eventually form roughly triangular clumps. 'Though I do plant in groups, I also have odd plants dotted about here and there to look as though they had seeded themselves, so that right from the start the bed isn't too regulated, as though I had painted it by numbers!'

Rosemary Verey also believes that it's very important, occasionally, to break her own rules. 'Something I try to do, if someone gives me a plant or I buy one on impulse, is ask myself, "Where would it be quite absurd to put it?", and put it there! So I might put a tall plant at the front of a border. In fact, I did plant a climbing golden honeysuckle (*Lonicera japonica* 'Aureo-reticulata') at the front of the border where it is spilling out all over the path – trailing rather than climbing. I've also done it the other way round and got a semi-prostrate plant, *Verbena* × *hybrida* 'Sissinghurst', to climb up a wall!'

The white flowering cherry *Prunus* 'Tai Haku' is the 'star' of this bed in spring, but the background foliage plants are attractive all year.

The fact that you allow space on your planting plan for large clumps of herbaceous perennials doesn't necessarily mean that you have to buy three or even five of everything to start with if the budget doesn't allow. Buy one large plant and, if it's suitable, either divide it up carefully into two or three smaller ones right away or grow it in your border for a season and then divide it up to make three or even more new plants. Obviously in the first year that will mean plenty of wide-open spaces in the border, but you can easily fill them with annuals, also planted in bold drifts or clumps and not dotted about the border like currants in a bun!

Above: The vivid blue of *Campanula grandis* against the foliage of the golden mock orange (*Philadelphus coronarius* 'Aureus') is a simple but very effective contrast.

Left: In winter evergreen foliage, bare twigs and dried flower heads, all rimed with frost, provide a very subtle colour scheme.

How Near? How Far?

One reason for learning a bit about plants, and particularly how tall they'll grow and how widely they'll spread, is to make sure that, when you're planning and planting your border, you get the spacing right for the permanent plants – the shrubs and the trees. It is very hard for first time gardeners, confronted with all that bare earth, to believe that a small container-grown shrub, only 30–40 cm (about 1 ft) high, which they're about to plant will make a bush covering an area 1.5 × 1.5 m (5 × 5 ft) in five years' time, and 3 × 3 m (10 × 10 ft) in ten years, and to leave that amount of space for it.

While it would be daft to leave only about 60 m (2 ft) between it and its neighbouring shrub – they would be fighting each other within two or three years for space, food and light – it would be a little unrealistic in a small garden to leave an area 3 m (10 ft) across totally bare. What you could do in that situation is plant in between the permanent subjects relatively short-lived shrubs, like broom (*Cytisus*), or shrubs that aren't totally hardy, like the rock rose (*Cistus*), which would be killed off in a really cold winter. Alternatively, you could use herbaceous plants for the same purpose or even some of the taller-growing annuals, like mallow (*Lavatera trimestris*), Shirley or Iceland poppies, or gloriosa daises (*Rudbeckia*).

Where to Buy Your Plants

You might think that buying your plants is the easiest part of making a garden – you simply go to a first-class garden centre where the staff are really knowledgeable and helpful, and where there is a wide range of healthy, well-grown, well-cared-for, clearly labelled plants. But in practice it isn't that simple, for not every garden centre is first-class. It's not always easy to judge by appearances either. Some rather small, basic, old-fashioned garden centres may have an excellent range of really well-grown shrubs, while some spanking new, architect-designed, out-of-town ones may have a wider selection of silk flowers or fudge than they have, say, of clematis!

The only way to tell is to look at the plants. Do they look healthy? Obviously, if a plant is visibly diseased, the pot is full of weeds and moss, and there is a tangle of fibrous roots showing through the hole in the bottom, it's been there a long time and hasn't been well looked after, so leave it where it is. Equally, you want shrubs or trees that are container-grown, not 'containerised' – grown in open ground, dug up and potted just before they're put on sale. The best way to tell is to pick up the plant carefully by its top growth. If the pot comes too, it's well rooted and you know it's container-grown. If the plant starts to come out of the compost, it's probably 'containerised' and will take longer to establish in the ground once you plant it out. Trees should be well-shaped – your homework will have told you what a particular tree ought to look like – and balanced. If it's lop-sided, leave it alone.

When it comes to buying shrubs, small is beautiful. Look at all the shrubs on offer of the particular variety you want and pick the one with the best shape and the bushiest growth, which almost always means that it won't be the biggest. Avoid buying climbers, like clematis or honeysuckle, with long, bare stems – you'll have to cut them back anyway, as they won't produce new growth or flowers on those stems – and look for plants with plenty of new shoots coming from the base. Herbaceous plants aren't such a problem, because as long as they are actually showing some signs of life, they will grow perfectly well once they're planted out.

If you're not happy with the range or quality of plants on sale at your local garden centre, it's well worth finding out which is the nearest good garden centre and making a special journey. After all, you want your trees and shrubs to last a lifetime, so it's worth making sure you start off with the best money can buy. *Which?* publishes *The Good Gardener's Guide*, which contains details of and inspectors' reports on garden centres all over the British Isles. If you don't want to buy it (it costs £7.95), the chances are your local reference library will have a copy.

The *Guide* also contains comprehensive lists of nurseries which specialise in particular plants – alpines, for example, fuchsias or fruit trees – many of which will supply plants by mail order. Certainly if you want something slightly out of the ordinary, that's the way to buy it. Most garden centres stock perhaps twenty different varieties of clematis if you're lucky. A specialist like Treasures of Tenbury Wells supplies over 200! The drawback with buying plants by mail order is, of course, that you can't see what you're buying, and since many nurseries despatch plants solely during the dormant season, it requires an act of faith to believe that the pots you receive which seem to contain only bits of dead growth and compost really are healthy herbaceous perennials that will burgeon forth in the spring! Provided you stick to reputable firms experienced in mail order, who are happy to replace any plants that arrive damaged, you shouldn't have any problems. Always remember that you get what you pay for. If a newspaper small ad. offers you plants at unbelievably low prices, they are almost bound to be miniscule rooted cuttings which are very difficult to get established. You should also stay well clear of small ads. offering a 'new' or 'miracle' plant that will solve all your gardening problems at a stroke, especially if they don't give its proper botanical name.

CHAPTER THREE

Trees

The trees you choose to plant will almost certainly be the largest living features in your borders, and to some extent will dictate the rest of the planting, so it is very important to choose the right trees and plant them in the right place. In a small garden you should choose small trees – you only have to drive through any suburb and see the semis, like Sleeping Beauty's castle, hidden behind huge weeping willows or gigantic monkey puzzle trees to realise how vital that choice is, not only for you, but also for future generations!

There are comparatively few trees that are truly small – in most encyclopaedias of trees and shrubs 'small trees' are defined as those reaching at least 10 m (33 ft) when they're fully grown – but they do exist and it's well worth seeking them out. Several species of popular trees have dwarf relatives – the weeping Kilmarnock willow (*Salix caprea* 'Pendula'), for example, is a very attractive, small, umbrella-shaped tree which seldom reaches more than 2–3 m (6–10 ft) in height, whereas its much more widely known relation, the golden weeping willow (*Salix* × *chrysocoma*), can eventually reach 25 m (80 ft) and do unspeakable things to your drains and foundations in the process.

In a very small garden you're unlikely to have room for more than two or three trees, so finding the right position for them is essential. Since they're going to be the tallest plants in your garden, and since you will certainly choose particularly attractive specimens, they will draw the eye, so you must make sure that they will draw it to where you want it to look. In the first time garden, for instance, we planted the very pretty ornamental crab apple, *Malus* 'Profusion', in the corner diagonally opposite the patio doors. That was part of the overall design, intended to swing the axis of the garden from the much shorter front-to-back axis to the diagonal one across the garden, and make the plot seem larger.

You can also use trees to screen a blot on the landscape. If you have a view of, say, an electricity pylon in the distance or an ugly tower block, a carefully sited tree can be used either to mask it completely or, if that's not possible, to conceal it partially and distract your eye so that you don't notice it quite as much. The best place to put your tree in this instance is not necessarily right on your boundary. To work out the ideal position you will need a pole 2 m (6 ft 6 in) long – a hoe or even a broom handle will do – and an assistant whose hand is about 2 m (6 ft 6 in) above the ground

The paperbark maple
(*Acer griseum*).

when he/she stretches an arm above his/her head, which will give you a height of about 4 m (13 ft) in total. Tie a handkerchief or similar-sized piece of cloth to the end of the pole.

Then sit where you think you will be spending most time looking at the view – the sunniest spot in the garden or even inside the house by the patio doors – and get your assistant to stand directly between you and the pylon or tower block, pole in hand, arm extended, and walk slowly away from you towards it. When the handkerchief or cloth appears to be level with the top of the eyesore, you know that a tree like the Tibetan cherry (*Prunus serrula*) planted in that spot will be helping to screen it within five years since it grows to about 4 × 2 m (13 × 6 ft 6 in) in that length of time, and when it's fully mature, some twenty years on, it will still be only about 7 × 4 m (24 × 13 ft).

It may be, of course, that to screen the eyesore effectively the tree ought to be planted in your neighbour's garden. If you're prepared to choose something that will suit both your purposes, to pay for it and plant it, you may find your neighbour is more than happy to oblige. Incidentally, you should never plant vigorous trees closer to the house than 12 m (40 ft) away. Not only can their roots cause damage to drains but, more seriously they can cause soil shrinkage, which can damage the foundations and lead in turn to cracking and subsidence – extremely expensive problems to put right.

What Tree?

Where space is at a premium, the trees and shrubs you choose really have to earn their keep. You can't afford to choose something that is lovely for a couple of weeks, and then for the rest of the season is just plain dull.

You want a tree with as many appealing qualities as you can get – very attractive new foliage, striking autumn colour, interesting variegated or coloured foliage through the summer, flowers, berries, superb bark, a good strong shape against the sky in winter. It's worth making a check list and even awarding points to see which trees are going to give the best value. The shape of the tree is well worth thinking about. One with a broad head and large leaves, like some members of the maple family – *Acer platanoides*, for instance – will create dense shade beneath it while a mountain ash (*Sorbus aucuparia*) with a much more open head and feathery leaves will provide the sort of dappled shade in which many plants thrive.

Talking of shade, aspect isn't such an important factor in your choice of trees as it is in the choice of most other plants. In the majority of gardens trees will soon grow above the shadows cast by garden walls and fences, so unless it's shaded by the house, of course, a tree in a north-facing border will get as much sun as in one facing south. Obviously, if your garden is in the shadow of tall buildings or large overhanging trees, any trees you plant won't grow into the sun, or at least not for a very long time, so bear that in mind when making your choice. In the lists of suitable trees that follow, all will thrive in sun or light shade, and those that will grow happily in a more shady spot are labelled accordingly.

Many trees will grow well in several different soil types, but they are listed in each category where appropriate, so that if you have a sandy soil, for example, you'll find our complete selection of suitable trees under that heading. Almost all the trees that will grow in clay, chalky soil and sandy soil will also do as well – if not better – in the elusive, slightly acid medium loam, so under that heading are listed those few small trees that will *only* give of their best in a good, rich, well-drained slightly acid loam.

Trees for Clay Soils

FOR VERY WET, HEAVY SOILS
'Golden' grey alder (*Alnus incana* 'Aurea') has soft golden leaves and stems and red-tinged catkins in spring. Its leaves become more green in the summer, but it has good autumn colour. Like many golden-leafed trees and shrubs, it's better grown in light shade, as hot, midday sun can scorch its leaves.

Approx. height and spread after five years 3 × 1.5 m (10 × 5 ft); after twenty years 11.5 × 3.5 m (38 × 12 ft).

Silver willow (*Salix alba sericea,* also known as *S.a. argentea*) makes a small, round-headed tree with long, slender, silvery leaves. In winter its bare stems form a delicate tracery against the sky. It responds well to pruning.

Approx. height and spread (if unpruned) after five years 3 × 1.5 m (10 × 5 ft); after twenty years 5 × 2.5 m (16 × 8 ft).

FOR MOIST CLAY SOILS

Maples (*Acer* species)

Paperbark maple (*Acer griseum*) is a near-perfect tree for a small garden because it has so many good qualities – attractive, orange-buff foliage in spring, glorious red and scarlet autumn colour, and in winter, on wood that's at least three years old, the orange-brown bark peels away to reveal new cinnamon-coloured bark beneath. Added to which, its ascending branches and rather open habit allow light to reach plants growing beneath it. It's also very slow-growing.

Approx. height and spread after five years 2 × 1.2 m (6 × 4 ft); after twenty years 6 × 3 m (20 × 10 ft).

Snake-bark maple (*Acer capillipes*) is another small tree whose bark – grey-green with white veining – is one of its most attractive features. Its fresh green leaves have a reddish tinge in spring and turn a fiery orange-red in autumn.

Approx. height and spread after five years 3 × 1.5 m (10 × 5 ft); after twenty years 7 × 5 m (23 × 16 ft).

Acer negundo **'Flamingo'** has leaves which are pink when they open and then turn green and white with a pink flush which gradually fades as they mature. The brightest and most attractive colouring is on new growth, so ideally the tree should be pruned every year, but since it can be quite difficult to prune something 4–5 m (13–16 ft) tall, it is certainly easier to grow it as a shrub. Many nurseries supply it in both forms.

Average approx. height and spread (unpruned) after five years 3 × 2 m (10 × 6 ft); after twenty years 6 × 5 m (20 × 16 ft).

Acer pseudoplatanus **'Brilliantissimum'** is a very slow-growing small tree about which opinions are sharply divided. Some people love its foliage, which opens deep shrimp-pink in spring, becoming paler flesh pink, then creamy-yellow and pale green before assuming its summer mid-green, and don't mind that it's actually rather dull for the rest of the season. Others think the spring pyrotechnics don't actually compensate for its lack of interest during the rest of the year. It's a matter of taste.

Approx. height and spread after five years 2.5 × 1.5 m (8 × 5 ft); after twenty years 4.5 × 3.5 m ($14\frac{1}{2}$ × 12 ft).

The Japanese ornamental crab (*Malus floribunda*).

Flowering thorn (*Crataegus oxycantha* 'Paul's Double Scarlet', also known as *C.o.* 'Coccinea Plena') makes a small, round-headed tree and has dark pinky-red double flowers in late spring and early summer. It bears a few small, red berries in the autumn. Less widely available, though very attractive, is the double pink-flowered variety *C.o.* 'Rosea Plena'.

Approx. height and spread after five years 4 × 1.2 m (13 × 4 ft); after twenty years 6 × 6 m (20 × 20 ft).

Golden chain tree (*Laburnum × watereri* 'Vossii') has masses of bright golden flowers hanging in long bunches in May and June. Its green bark is also an attractive feature and its sharply ascending branches mean that you can usually grow plants underneath since they will get plenty of light. The only drawback with laburnum is that every part of it – not only the seeds – is poisonous, so it's not a tree to choose if you have small children or are planning to have some.

Approx. height and spread after five years 4 × 2 m (13 × 6 ft); after twenty years 7 × 5 m (23 × 16 ft).

Ornamental crab apples (*Malus* species)
You really are spoilt for choice here because so many varieties of ornamental crab are excellent for small gardens, what with masses

Malus 'Profusion'.

of flowers in spring, in some cases attractively hued foliage, and bright-coloured fruits in autumn.

Japanese crab (*Malus floribunda*) is a stunning sight in spring when it has deep red buds, newly opened pale pink flowers and more mature blush-white ones all at the same time. It has a semi-weeping habit, and branches on mature specimens can almost reach the ground, as though they are bowed down under the weight of the flowers! In autumn it has small, cherry-like fruits.
Approx. height and spread after five years 4 × 1.5 m (13 × 5 ft); after twenty years 8 × 6 m (26 × 20 ft).

Malus hupehensis also flowers abundantly, and as a bonus its white flowers, which are pink in bud, are scented. In autumn it has small yellow fruits flushed with red.
Approx. height and spread after five years 3 × 1.2 m (10 × 4 ft); after twenty years 6 × 4 m (20 × 13 ft).

Malus sargentii is one of the smallest crabs. It has masses of scented white flowers (tinted yellow in bud) with golden stamens. In autumn it bears bright red, currant-like fruits and its leaves turn yellow.
Approx. height and spread after five years 1.5 m × 70 cm (5 × 2½ ft); after twenty years 5 × 2 m (16 × 6 ft).

Malus 'Simcoe', a small but strong-growing tree, has coppery young foliage, large, purplish-pink flowers in abundance and purplish-red fruits in autumn.
Approx. height and spread after five years 2.5 × 1.5 m (8 × 5 ft); after twenty years 4.5 × 2.5 m (15 × 8 ft).

Malus 'Golden Hornet' has white flowers, followed by bright yellow fruits in autumn. For some reason birds prefer red and orange fruits to yellow, so these get left until well into the winter when everything else has gone. It's also useful as a pollinator for apple trees.
Approx. height and spread after five years 4 × 1.5 m (13 × 5 ft); after twenty years 8 × 6 m (26 × 20 ft).

Malus 'John Downie' is more upright in habit than 'Golden Hornet', has pink-budded white flowers and plenty of large orange fruits flushed with red which are the best for making jelly or wine.
Approx. height and spread after five years 4 × 1.5 m (13 × 5 ft); after twenty years 8 × 6 m (26 × 20 ft).

Malus 'Red Jade' is a small, weeping crab which has bright green leaves that turn yellow in autumn and blush-white flowers followed by small, bright red fruits.
Approx. height and spread after five years 2 × 1.5 m (6 × 5 ft); after twenty years 3 × 5 m (10 × 16 ft).

Malus 'Maypole'. This is one of a brand new breed of columnar trees introduced in the summer of 1989 and marketed under the name 'Ballerina trees' which are ideal for a confined space since they reach a height of only 2.5 m (8 ft) and a spread of about 30 cm (1 ft) in five years. 'Maypole' has purple-tinged foliage, cerise-pink flowers and a good crop of dark red fruits in autumn. It also has three columnar cousins – 'Waltz', 'Polka' and 'Bolero' – which are surprisingly heavy-cropping garden apples – early-flowering, mid-season and late respectively – and though we are not covering fruit trees in this book in any detail, these are well worth mentioning because they need no pruning and so are extremely easy to look after. Although they are partially self-fertile, they will produce a much better crop if you plant two different varieties, and the ornamental crab 'Maypole' will pollinate all the rest.
Approx. height and spread after five years 2.5 m × 30 cm (8 × 1 ft); after twenty years – impossible to say, since they haven't been around that long.

The following *Malus* hybrids are recommended for their coloured foliage:
Malus 'Liset' has glossy, deep red leaves, deep crimson flowers and oxblood-red fruits.

Malus 'Profusion' has coppery-crimson young foliage which slowly turns green, purplish-red flowers which fade to pink, and oxblood-red fruits.

Malus 'Royalty' is considered by some to be the best purple-leafed form since its wine-coloured foliage keeps its glossiness until it falls. It has large, mid-pink flowers and wine-red fruits.

Approx. height and spread after five years 4 × 1.5 m (13 × 5 ft); after twenty years 8 × 6 m (26 × 20 ft).

Flowering cherries, plums and peaches (*Prunus* species)

This species offers an even wider choice than the ornamental crabs, though you need to stop yourself being seduced by some of the spectacular, double-flowered varieties, like the 'boudoir' pink *Prunus* 'Kanzan', that you often see in streets and parks – the best place for them, some would say. Make sure that you choose one which will still have something to offer once the flowers have fallen after just a week or so and you've swept sackfuls of sugar-pink petals off the lawn.

Some breeders are now offering Japanese flowering cherries grafted on to dwarfing rootstocks, which means the final height and spread of the tree is reduced. Instead of P. 'Taoyoma Zakura' ending up at 7 × 7 m (23 × 23 ft) after twenty years, for example, it will reach only about 5 × 5 m (16 × 16 ft). It's worth checking with the garden centre before you buy on which sort of rootstock your tree is grafted.

Purple-leafed plum (*Prunus cerasifera* 'Nigra') is at its best in spring when the new blood-red foliage provides a dramatic contrast to the pale pink flowers which appear at the same time, or even sometimes slightly before it. The foliage gradually darkens to purple through the summer.

Approx. height and spread after five years 3 × 1.5 m (10 × 5 ft); after twenty years 8 × 4 m (26 × 13 ft).

Prunus **'Accolade'** is a superb small tree with a graceful, open, spreading habit. In early April its clusters of deep pink buds open into semi-double, hanging, light pink flowers up to 4 cm ($1\frac{1}{2}$ in) across with fringed petals. It goes on flowering for weeks.

Approx. height and spread after five years 3.5 × 3 m (12 × 10 ft); after twenty years 8 × 8 m (26 × 26 ft).

Yoshino cherry (*Prunus* × *yedoensis*) also makes a graceful small tree with arching branches and masses of almond-scented, blush-white flowers in late March-early April. It also has good autumn colour.

Approx. height and spread after five years 3 × 2 m (10 × 6 ft); after twenty years 7 × 5 m (23 × 16 ft).

Sargent's cherry (*Prunus sargentii*) in autumn.

Sargent's cherry (*Prunus sargentii*), which eventually forms a rather flat-topped tree, scores on several counts. Not only does it have masses of single pink flowers in early spring, but its new leaves are coppery red when they first appear, turning first green, then, as early as September in some areas, brilliant vermilion and scarlet.
Approx. height and spread after five years 3.5 × 2.5 m (12 × 8 ft); after twenty years 9 × 10 m (30 × 32 ft).

Korean hill cherry 'Autumn Glory' (*Prunus serrulata pubescens* 'Autumn Glory') also scores heavily on several counts, with bronze-tinged new foliage, single white flowers and stunning autumn tints – deep purples and reds. It forms a spreading, dome-shaped tree and in winter its somewhat twisted stems make a delicate tracery against the sky.
Approx. height and spread after five years 2.5 × 2 m (8 × 6 ft); after twenty years 8 × 9 m (26 × 30 ft).

Tibetan cherry (*Prunus serrula*) has masses of small white flowers in May, but its main claim to fame is its superb, mahogany-coloured bark which peels away to reveal a surface as smooth and polished as that of fine antique furniture. It takes between five and ten years for this to develop.
Approx. height and spread after five years 4 × 2 m (13 × 6 ft); after twenty years 7 × 4 m (23 × 13 ft).

The weeping willow-leafed pear (*Pyrus salicifolia* 'Pendula').

Autumn cherry (*Prunus subhirtella* 'Autumnalis') in fact produces semi-double white flowers on bare stems from early autumn (November) intermittently right through the winter to April, depending on the weather. A really cold snap can delay the flowers, but a spell of mild weather will bring them out. It has quite good golden autumn colour too. There is also an attractive variety with pink flowers, *P.s.* 'Autumnalis Rosea'.

Approx. height and spread after five years 1.5 × 2 m (5 × 6 ft); after twenty years 7 × 7 m (23 × 23 ft).

Japanese flowering cherries (*Prunus serrulata*)

Lombardy cherry (*Prunus serrulata* 'Amanogawa') makes a tall, narrow column of pale candy-pink flowers in spring and its foliage turns gold and flame in autumn. It's a very popular choice for small gardens because it is so narrow.

Approx. height and spread after five years 3 × 1 m (10 × 3 ft); after twenty years 6 × 2.2 m (20 × 7 ft).

Prunus **'Shirotae'** or **'Mount Fuji'** has fragrant, single or semi-double pure white flowers, very attractive against the fresh, light green leaves with their distinctive fringed edges in spring. It forms a wide-spreading tree, and in mature specimens some of the horizontal branches may touch the ground.

Great white cherry (*Prunus* 'Tai Haku') produces single, pure white flowers up to 5 cm (2 in) across, which are set off by the coppery-red young foliage in mid-spring. The leaves, which are exceptionally large, turn first green, then red and gold in autumn.

Approx. height and spread (for both trees) after five years 3.5 × 2.5 m (12 × 8 ft); after twenty years 7 ×·7 m (23 × 23 ft).

Prunus 'Tao-yoma Zakura' is a small, slow-growing tree with a spreading habit. It has fragrant, semi-double, shell-pink flowers which fade to blush-white, and attractive coppery young foliage.
Approx. height and spread after five years 3 × 2 m (10 × 6 ft); after twenty years 7 × 7 m (23 × 23 ft).

Weeping cherries
Prunus × *yedoensis* 'Shidare Yoshino' has masses of pale pink flowers, fading to white, on branches that weep to the ground in early spring. *Prunus* × *yedoensis* 'Ivensii' has fragrant, snow-white flowers and a similar habit. They are not so easy to find as Cheal's weeping cherry (a name sometimes applied to *Prunus subhirtella* 'Pendula Rosea' and sometimes to *Prunus* 'Kitu Shidare Sakura'), but specialist nurseries have them and they are well worth the extra effort involved in finding them.
Approx. height and spread after five years 3 × 3 m (10 × 10 ft); after twenty years 5 × 6 m (16 × 20 ft).

Ornamental pears (*Pyrus* species)
Snow pear (*Pyrus nivalis*) takes its common name not only from the white flowers which it produces in abundance in spring, but also from the white 'wool' which covers the young leaves and shoots appearing at the same time. The foliage then becomes silver-grey. It's not widely available, but good specialist nurseries stock it.
Approx. height and spread after five years 3 × 2 m (10 × 6 ft); after twenty years 7 × 5 m (23 × 16 ft).

Willow-leafed pear (*Pyrus salicifolia* 'Pendula') has long, silvery willow-like leaves which are also covered in a silky white down until early summer. It does have small white flowers in April, but it is grown primarily for the silvery foliage it eventually forms.
Approx. height and spread after five years 2.5 × 2 m (8 × 6 ft); after twenty years 4 × 3 m (13 × 10 ft).

Rowan or mountain ash and whitebeam (*Sorbus* species)
Another family with many members worthy of garden room in a small plot, since they have flowers, pretty foliage, good autumn colour and berries.

Sorbus 'Joseph Rock' has clusters of small white flowers in spring and fresh green, feathery foliage which turns copper and gold in autumn when its yellow berries appear. Though it's a pyramid shape when young, its branches become more steeply ascending with age and it finally forms a tight, neat head. Look out, too, for S. 'Embley', which has superb autumn colour.
Approx. height and spread after five years 2.5 × 1.5 m (8 × 5 ft); after twenty years 10 × 5 m (32 × 16 ft).

Kashmir mountain ash (*Sorbus cashmiriana*) is a stunning little tree, with very pale pink flowers in spring and beautiful, fern-like foliage which turns red in autumn. Its hanging clusters of pearl-white berries stay on the tree until well into the winter. It has a more open habit than 'Joseph Rock'.
Approx. height and spread after five years 2×2 m (6×6 ft); after twenty years 4×4 m (13×13 ft).

Sorbus vilmorinii makes a slightly larger tree than *S. cashmiriana*, but has similar white flowers in spring and delicate ferny foliage which turns purplish-red in autumn. Its berries, which hang in clusters, start out a rosy red then fade slowly to pink, blush-white and finally white.
Approx. height and spread after five years 2.5×1.5 m (8×5 ft); after twenty years 6×3 m (20×10 ft).

Sorbus sargentiana comes into its own in autumn and winter when its large and attractive leaves, up to 30 cm (1 ft) long, take on superb autumn colour. It also has bright red fruits which are then replaced by large crimson buds, sticky like a horse chestnut's, on pale creamy-green stems.
Approx. height and spread after five years 2.5×1.5 m (8×5 ft); after twenty years 6×3 m (20×10 ft).

Whitebeam (*Sorbus aria* 'Lutescens') is a picture in the spring when it has white flowers and its new, silvery foliage is covered in creamy down. The leaves turn grey-green on top and grey below, which creates an attractive effect when the wind disturbs them. It sometimes has red-orange berries in autumn. If you can find its near-relative, *S.* 'Mitchellii', snap it up. Its leaves are twice the size and quite dramatic in spring.
Approx. height and spread after five years 3×2 m (10×6 ft); after twenty years 12×8 m (39×26 ft).

Trees for Chalky Soils

Chalky soils are usually rather shallow, which means choosing trees that are not particularly deep-rooting, and since they are also alkaline, it means that lime haters, like the Canadian maples or the sweet gum (*Liquidambar styraciflua*), won't thrive. Even so, there are plenty of attractive trees to choose from.

Maples (*Acer* species)
Acer negundo 'Flamingo': see under 'Trees for Clay Soils'.
Acer pseudoplatanus 'Brilliantissimum': see under 'Trees for Clay Soils'.

Birches (*Betula* species)

Although our native silver birch (*Betula pendula*) is very beautiful, it's perhaps at its best grown with others in a group, and a very small garden simply doesn't have room for a copse! Incidentally, birches don't transplant well, so if you do want one of these trees buy a container-grown specimen, not a bare-rooted one.

Swedish birch (*Betula pendula* 'Dalecarlica') has deep-cut, feathery, light green foliage which turns yellow in autumn and, combined with its horizontal branches and hanging twigs, gives it an airy, delicate effect. Its stems soon become white.

Approx. height and spread after five years 6×1.5 m $(20 \times 5$ ft); after twenty years 12×5 m $(39 \times 16$ ft).

Purple-leafed birch (*Betula pendula* 'Purpurea') makes a smaller tree, with bright purple foliage in spring, which slowly ages to dark green, and purple catkins in winter.

Approx. height and spread after five years 4×1 m $(13 \times 3$ ft); after twenty years 8×2 m $(26 \times 6$ ft).

Himalayan birch (*Betula jacquemontii*) stands out for its dazzling white stems under the peeling brown bark. It also has good autumn colour and large catkins in winter.

Approx. height and spread after five years 6×1.5 m $(20 \times 5$ ft); after twenty years 12×5 m $(39 \times 16$ ft).

Laburnum × *watereri* 'Vossii': see under 'Trees for Clay Soils'.

Malus species: see under 'Trees for Clay Soils'.

Prunus species: see under 'Trees for Clay Soils'.

Pyrus species: see under 'Trees for Clay Soils'.

Golden false acacia (*Robinia pseudacacia* 'Frisia') will grow happily in chalky soil as long as it has been enriched with organic matter and is neither too thin nor too alkaline. It has wonderful feathery golden foliage, which appears quite late in the spring, and an attractive, open habit. Its branches are rather brittle, so it needs a spot sheltered from the wind. It is also notoriously difficult to get established, so always buy container-grown trees and make sure you plant it in the right place first time round!

Approx. height and spread after five years 3×2 m $(10 \times 6$ ft); after twenty years 12×6 m $(39 \times 20$ ft).

Whitebeam (*Sorbus aria* 'Lutescens'): see under 'Trees for Clay Soils'.

The Himalayan birch (*Betula jacquemontii*) in winter.

Trees for Sandy Soils

Although they have many of the same qualities as chalky soils, and some of the same trees will grow quite happily in them, some sandy soils are likely to be acid, or at least less alkaline, so there are additional trees that will tolerate them.

Maples (*Acer* species)
Acer griseum; *Acer negundo* 'Flamingo'; *Acer pseudoplatanus* 'Brilliantissimum': see under 'Trees for Clay Soils'.

Snowy mespilus (*Amelanchier lamarckii*) is another superb small tree. It is smothered in small, white flowers in spring at the same time as the new leaves appear, tinged with bronze. In autumn these turn brilliant orange-red and, though the tree will grow on a slightly

alkaline soil, the colouring is far better on an acid soil.
Approx. height and spread after five years 4 × 3 m (13 × 10 ft); after twenty years 7.5 × 6 m (25 × 20 ft).

Birches (*Betula* species): see under 'Trees for Clay Soils'.

Katsura tree (*Cercidiphyllum japonicum*) is a fine tree with heart-shaped leaves which open a purplish-pink, turn first a sea-green in summer and then shades of smoky pink, red and yellow in autumn. Although it will grow on sandy soil, the more organic matter you have added (in other words, the richer the soil), the larger it will grow and the better the autumn colour. It dislikes windy conditions, so make sure that you find it a sheltered spot.
Approx. height and spread after five years 5 × 3 m (16 × 10 ft); after twenty years 10 × 7 m (32 × 23 ft).

Golden honey locust (*Gleditsia triacanthos* 'Sunburst') has beautiful, bright golden, feathery foliage and, though round-topped when young, it will eventually make an upright tree. Again, the more organic matter you have worked into the soil, the more it will thrive. It's one of the easiest-to-grow golden foliage trees.
Approx. height and spread after five years 3 × 1.5 m (10 × 5 ft); after twenty years 7 × 5 m (23 × 16 ft).

Trees for Slightly Acid, Medium Loam

Almost all the trees already listed in the preceding sections will grow in slightly acid, medium loam, so the following are subjects which will only do really well in this type of soil.

Golden Indian bean tree (*Catalpa bignonioides* 'Aurea') has the most beautiful, large, velvety, gold leaves which have a coppery tinge as they unfurl and keep their freshness throughout the summer. It is very slow-growing and eventually produces a small, spreading tree, as broad as it is high; or, if it's cut back regularly, it makes a stunning shrub. You can buy trees grafted on to a 1.5 or 2 m (5 or 6 ft) stem, to give height immediately.
Approx. height and spread after five years 1.5 × 1.5 m (5 × 5 ft); after twenty years 5 × 5 m (16 × 16 ft).

CHAPTER FOUR

North-facing borders

Many new gardeners are daunted by the prospect of a shady, north-facing border. A sunny, south-facing one seems to present far fewer problems – roses will do well, so will delphiniums, poppies, daisies and, of course, any number of bright, cheerful, easy-to-grow annuals. But what do you plant under that north-facing wall where the sun seldom shines, or under those tall, over-hanging trees?

The truth is that there are many absolutely superb plants which will only give of their best in a shady spot. With a few exceptions, like some of the primula family, the stunning blue poppy (*Meconopsis betonicifolia*) and some golden foliage plants like the golden elder (*Sambucus nigra* 'Aurea'), the shade lovers are not as showy, not as brightly coloured as the sun-loving brigade, but theirs is a more subtle, quieter charm that remains appealing for longer.

Many shade-loving plants originate from moist, cool woodland, so their colours are paler – soft primrose yellow, pale pink, mauve and blue, as well as white – than those whose natural habitat is bright sunlight. They also tend to have large leaves to make the most of the available light which is needed in the plant's food-manufacturing process, and it's in the shady border that many plants, grown as much for their foliage as their flowers really thrive – subjects such as plantain lilies (*Hosta* species), elephant's ears (*Bergenia* species), lungwort (*Pulmonaria* species), dead nettle (*Lamium maculatum*).

Foliage is particularly important in a shady border since many woodlanders flower in spring before the trees come into leaf and take most of the light, and so you will be relying on foliage to provide a lot of summer colour and interest.

The use of shrubs and herbaceous plants with variegated foliage – the much-maligned green-and-gold-spotted laurel (*Aucuba japonica* 'Variegata'), for example, or the gold-splashed ivy (*Hedera helix* 'Goldheart'), or the golden elder or Bowles' golden grass (*Milium effusum* 'Aureum') with their plain golden foliage – really

Key to plan of the Barnsdale garden on moist soil (*opposite*)

1. *Hydrangea petiolaris*
2. *Lonicera tellmanniana*
3. *Hedera helix* 'Goldheart'
4. *Lonicera periclymenum* 'Serotina'
5. *Rosa bonica*
6. *Solanum crispum* 'Glasnevin'
7. Rose 'Alberic Barbier' and *Clematis viticella* 'Etoile Violette'
8. Clematis 'Comtesse de Bouchard'
9. *Actinidia kolomikta*
10. Rose 'Pink Perpetue' and Clematis *Jackmanii Superba*
11. Rose 'Mermaid'
12. *Prunus* 'Pink Shell'
13. *Sorbus cashmiriana*
14. *Malus* 'Profusion'
15. *Eleagnus pungens* 'Maculata'
16. *Berberis thunbergii* 'Aurea'
17. *Mahonia* 'Charity'
18. *Weigela florida* 'Variegata'
19. *Photinia × frazerii* 'Red Robin'
20. *Sopraea × bumalda* 'Goldflame'
21. *Viburnum davidii*
22. *Rosa rubrifolia*
23. Fuchsia 'Tom Thumb'
24. *Skimmia japonica* 'Rubella'
25. *Philadelphus coronarius* 'Aureus'
26. *Cotinus coggygria* 'Atropurpurea'
27. *Chamaecyparis lawsoniana* 'Pottenii'
28. *Chamaecyparis lawsoniana* 'Minima Aurea'
29. *Juniperus squamata* 'Blue Star'
30. *Buddleia fallowiana alba*
31. *Artemisia* 'Powis Castle'.
32. *Delphinium* hybrids
33. *Anthemis cupaniana*
34. *Stachys olympicum* 'Primrose Heron'
35. *Coreopsis verticillata* 'Moonbeam'
36. Lupin 'Russell Hybrids'
37. *Alstromeria* 'Princess'
38. *Allium schoenoprasum* 'Forescate'
39. *Choysia ternata* 'Sundance'
40. *Dianthus deltoides*
41. *Saponaria ocymoides*
42. *Ajuga* 'Burgundy Glow'
43. *Bergenia* 'Ballawley'
44. *Campanula lactiflora*
45. *Cimicifuga simplex*
46. *Rheum* 'Ace of Hearts'
47. *Hosta* 'Honeybells'
48. *Hosta* 'Buckshaw Blue'
49. *Hosta fortunei* 'Aurea'
50. *Brunnera macrophylla*
51. *Heuchera* 'Palace Purple'
52. Bowles' golden grass
53. *Viola labradorica*
54. *Rodgersia podophylla*
55. *Geranium nodosum*
56. *Viburnum juddii*
57. *Corylopsis pauciflora*
58. *Liriope muscari*
59. *Hedera helix hibernica*
60. *Penstemon* 'Garnet'
61. *Viola cornuta*
62. *Lilium regale*

White Turk's-cap lilies (*Lilium martagon* 'Album') above plants with superb foliage like *Astrantia major*, the wine-red *Heuchera* 'Palace Purple' and the steel-blue *Hosta* 'Halcyon'.

does seem to create a patch of sunshine in the shade. But plants with variegated and coloured foliage need enough plain greens around to point up the contrast and show them off to full advantage.

The actual design of the border is a matter of personal taste, but in this instance, since you are using plants which grow informally in their natural setting, it's probably better to adopt a similar informal style. Neat rows just wouldn't look right.

Identify Your Shade Type

There are several different types of shade. There's dappled shade beneath overhanging trees, which varies between shafts of sunlight and very little light of any description, depending on how the branches move; and then there's the shade found in the lee of north-facing walls, fences or tall buildings, where you may get practically no sunlight at all but a reasonable amount of light nonetheless.

There's also moist shade, in which most shade lovers will thrive, and then there's dry shade – usually under a dense canopy of trees, which prevents any rain reaching the soil beneath while they are in leaf and, in addition, the trees' roots greedily suck any available moisture out of the ground. Dry shade is one of the most difficult to plant successfully, but there are a number of attractive plants, like lady's mantle (*Alchemilla mollis*), foxgloves (*Digitalis* species) and ivy (*Hedera helix*), that will grow happily even there.

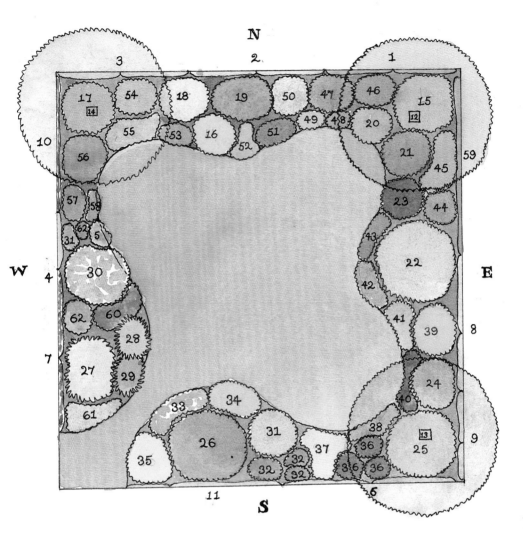

Soil

The type of soil you have isn't as important for shrubs and herbaceous plants as it is for trees. Most shrubs and herbaceous plants
are much more shallow-rooting than trees, and so it is possible,
with some hard work, to make a deep enough layer of clay soil
sufficiently well drained or a deep enough layer of sandy soil
sufficiently water-retentive to grow many of the same plants.

What is an important factor is whether the soil is acid or
alkaline. There are quite a few shade-loving plants that will grow
only on an acid soil. They might just tick over on a neutral soil,
but no more than that, and on a limy soil they will simply die.
Certainly, you can make a limy soil more water-retentive, and you
can reduce its alkalinity a little by adding masses of acid organic

matter (peat, leaf mould and so on), but you can never make it sufficiently acid to grow lime-hating plants. Since it's important to know which those plants are, they're listed separately. There are also a few plants that really do well only on chalk, but they are almost all sun lovers and so not relevant here.

The majority of plants will thrive on a soil that is slightly acid to neutral, and a number of them will tolerate lime. A few of these plants will also tolerate extreme conditions, like very heavy, wet clay, for example, and very thin, sandy soil and very deep shade. They obviously won't do as well as they would in slightly better conditions, but in those situations beggars can't be choosers and we must just be very grateful for anything that puts on even a half-way decent show! These brave souls are listed separately at the end of this chapter.

Moist Shade – Acid Soil

The following plants *must* have an acid soil.

SHRUBS

Camellias. Perhaps because of *The Lady of the Camellias*, these exquisite flowering shrubs are often thought of as exotic and therefore tender, but in fact, as long as they are sheltered from icy north and east winds, they will grow very well in a north-facing border or in dappled shade. They produce masses of single, semi-double or double flowers in a whole range of colours from white through many shades of pink to blood-red, and even a few multi-colours like the pink-and-white-striped *Camellia japonica* 'Lady Vansittart'. They start flowering between February and April, depending on the variety, and keep their flowers for several weeks. Once the flowers have fallen, their elegant, glossy green leaves are attractive in their own right.

Good varieties include: white flowers – *Camellia japonica* 'Alba Plena'; pink flowers – the soft pink, semi-double *C.j.* 'Lady Clare', the clear, rich pink *C.j.* 'Leonard Messel' and perhaps the most widely grown and most popular of all *Camellia × williamsii* 'Donation', with an abundance of large, semi-double, clear pink flowers from February onwards; red flowers – the large, semi-double, deep crimson *C.j.* 'Mercury', and *C.j.* 'Adolphe Audusson' whose semi-double, blood-red flowers have conspicuous gold stamens.
Approx. height and spread of *japonica* types after five years 1 × 1 m (3 × 3 ft); after ten years 1.5 × 1.5 m (5 × 5 ft). *Williamsii* types grow larger – up to 3 × 1.5 m (10 × 5 ft).

Checkerberry or wintergreen (*Gaultheria procumbens*) is a creeping, low-growing evergreen, providing good ground cover under larger, acid-loving shrubs. It has oval, green leaves, small, white flowers in summer, and bright red berries in autumn and winter. The berries and leaves both have the medicinal scent of wintergreen. It doesn't like heavy clay soils.

Approx. height and spread after five and ten years 10 cm × 1 m (4 in × 3 ft).

Pernettya mucronata. Although this dwarf evergreen is less well known than many other acid-lovers, it is well worth considering for a shady border. It has very small, glossy, deep green leaves, masses of small, white flowers and the most beautiful berries in autumn, ranging in colour from pearly white through various shades of pink to red and purple. To ensure a good crop of berries, plant the shrubs in groups of three or four, making sure that there is at least one male among them. The sex of a pernettya is not instantly obvious, so ask at the garden centre for a guaranteed male form. Good varieties include: white berries – *Pernettya mucronata* 'Alba', 'Snow White'; pink berries – 'Sea Shell' (pale shell pink), 'Pink Pearl' (lilac-pink); red berries – 'Bell's Seedling' (dark red), 'Cherry Ripe' (bright red); purple berries – 'Mulberry Wine' (magenta ageing to deep purple).

Approx. height and spread after five years 50 × 80 cm ($1\frac{1}{2}$ × $2\frac{1}{2}$ ft); after ten years 80 cm × 1.2 m ($2\frac{1}{2}$ × 4 ft).

Pieris. These are perhaps the ideal evergreen shrubs for a very small garden because they really do earn their keep. In spring tassels of small white flowers, which are bell-shaped rather like those of lily-of-the-valley, open at the same time as the new foliage is coming through. The crowns of new, slender, spear-shaped leaves start out an almost unbelievably vivid shade of scarlet, slowly fading through pink, cream and pale green before acquiring their glossy summer mid-green. The clusters of small, red buds for next season's flowers, which form in the autumn, add brightness during the winter months.

There are many good varieties available, but look out for *Pieris formosa* 'Wakehurst', which has shorter, broader leaves than most but superb spring colour; *Pieris forestii* 'Forest Flame', one of the hardiest varieties, with particularly bright new foliage; and *Pieris japonica* 'Variegata' whose leaves are variegated with creamy white flushed with pink when they first open. The last named is more slow-growing than most and forms a smaller shrub – about two thirds the usual height and spread.

Approx. height and spread after five years 80 cm × 1 m ($2\frac{1}{2}$ × 3 ft); after ten years 1.5 × 2 m (5 × 6 ft).

Rhododendrons. These are without doubt among the most eye-catching of our flowering shrubs and there are literally hundreds of different ones to choose from. Most of them, though, grow much

The acid-loving *Pieris forestii* 'Forest Flame' in spring.

too large for a small garden and many have little more to offer in the way of interest once the large, brilliantly coloured flowers have faded. There are some excellent dwarf rhododendrons, however, worth considering for any border in dappled shade. Look out for 'Bluebird' with violet-blue flowers, 'Pink Drift' with lavender-pink flowers and aromatic, olive-green leaves, 'Scarlet Wonder' with trumpet-shaped, frilly, red flowers, and 'Moonstone' with rosy-crimson buds opening to a creamy pale primrose yellow. Also attractive is *Rhododendron yakushimanum* and its hybrids. *R. yakushimanum* itself is a stunner – not only does it have masses of rose-pink buds, opening to apple-blossom-pink flowers which slowly fade to white, but its foliage is striking too. Its long, narrow, leathery leaves are silvery when they first appear, turning a really dark, glossy green on top, with woolly, brown undersides. Its many hybrids – like 'Doc' (light pink, fading to white), 'Grumpy' (pale

yellow with a hint of pink, fading to white), 'Silver Sixpence' (creamy white with pale lemon spots) and 'Surrey Heath' (rose pink lightly tinged with orange) – have superb flowers in a range of striking colours, but none has the same beautiful foliage as the parent.
Approx. height and spread after five years 60 × 60 cm (2 × 2 ft); after ten years 80 cm × 1 m (2 × 3 ft).

Azaleas are members of the same family as rhododendrons. Some of the deciduous kinds have almost neon-bright flowers in shades of orange, yellow and pink, while the foliage provides good autumn colour. Look for 'Kosters Brilliant Red' (vivid orange-red), 'Gibraltar' (dark red buds opening to flame-orange with a yellow flash), 'Coronation Lady' (salmon-pink with a bright orange flare).
Approx. height and spread after five years 1 × 1 m (3 × 3 ft); after ten years 1.5 × 1.5 m (5 × 5 ft).

The evergreen azaleas make small, rounded shrubs that are smothered in flowers in spring. Good varieties include: 'Blue Danube' (blue-violet), 'Mother's Day' (semi-double, bright red), 'Blaauw's Pink' (salmon pink), 'Hinomayo' (clear pink) and 'Palestrina' (pure white).
Approx. height and spread after five years 60 × 60 cm (2 × 2 ft); after ten years 80 cm × 1 m ($2\frac{1}{2}$ × 3 ft).

OTHER PLANTS
There are very few herbaceous plants (or annuals or bulbs) which must have an acid soil to do well – most of those that dislike lime will grow happily in neutral to slightly acid soil.

An exception is the Himalayan blue poppy (*Meconopsis betonicifolia*) which needs a cool, rich, acid soil if it is to do more than flower once after several years and then die. Given the right conditions, though, it produces flowers of a stunning, rich sky-blue in summer, and grows to a height of 90–120 cm (3–4 ft).

Moist Shade – Average Soil
The following plants will thrive in moist shade on average soil – that is to say, clay soil whose drainage has been improved, medium loam and sandy soil which has been made more water-retentive, all of which are slightly acid to neutral. Some of these plants will tolerate lime and they are marked accordingly.

CLIMBERS
Clematis, which like their heads in the sun and their roots in the shade, can be suitable for north-facing walls or fences, though the majority do prefer a sunnier situation. They also do best in a limy

soil, but will grow well enough in a neutral or slightly acid soil.

Good large-flowered varieties to look for include the widely available 'Nelly Moser' whose pale pink-mauve petals are striped with a deeper pink; the mauve-pink, free-flowering 'Comtesse de Bouchaud'; the pure white 'Marie Boisselot'; and the lavender-blue 'Mrs Cholmondeley'. Small-flowered varieties also do well on north walls – not the extremely rampant *Clematis montana*, unless you have masses of space, but varieties of *C. alpina*, for instance, which have nodding blue and white flowers in spring and are marvellous growing through evergreen shrubs like firethorn (*Pyracantha*). The late-flowering *C. viticella* varieties, with small flowers in wine-red, purple or white, are also good for growing through other shrubs. Most varieties should either be pruned back hard in winter to encourage better flowering or, in the case of *C. alpina*, should simply be pruned to keep them within their allotted space.

Flowers Mar–Oct (depending on the variety). Approx. height and spread 3–5 m (10–16 ft).

Climbing hydrangea (*Hydrangea petiolaris*) is a marvellous climber for all soils, and for shade. It's worth growing simply for the masses of bright, fresh green leaves it produces each spring, but it also has large, flat heads of white flowers in early summer, which turn brown in autumn and remain, attractively, on the bare stems in winter.

Approx. height and spread after five years 1.5 × 2 m (5 × 6 ft); after ten years 3 × 4 m + (10 × 16 ft +).

Ivy (*Hedera* species) is probably the best evergreen climber for shade and tolerates all kinds of soil. One of the variegated kinds, like the small-leaved, bright gold and green 'Goldheart', or the much larger-leaved *Hedera colchica* 'Paddy's Pride', really would brighten up a dark wall or fence. If you want a plain green – as a background for variegated shrubs, perhaps – the glossy, dark green *H. helix* 'Hibernica' is ideal. Ivies are self-clinging, but may need some help when you first put them in.

Approx. height and spread after five years 4 × 4 m (13 × 13 ft); after ten years 5 × 5 m (16 × 16 ft).

Honeysuckles (*Lonicera* species) usually prefer sun (though, like clematis, they like their roots in moist shade) but a few varieties will thrive in shade. *Lonicera × tellmanniana* has rich yellow flowers, flushed with red in bud, while *Lonicera × americana* has very sweetly scented flowers in summer which open white and slowly fade to yellow, flushed with pink. The gold-netted Japanese honeysuckle (*L. japonica* 'Aureo-reticulata') isn't as vigorous as *L. × americana* but has attractive semi-evergreen foliage as well as sweetly scented, small, yellow flowers in summer.

Flowers Jun–Sept. Approx. height and spread 3.5 × 8 m (12 × 26 ft).

Roses usually need a sunny situation to do well, but there are several ramblers and climbers that will grow successfully on shady walls provided that they have a moist enough soil. Look for 'Morning Jewel' with bright pink flowers, the pearly, blush-white 'New Dawn', 'Pink Perpétue' with carmine pink flowers, the yellow-flowered 'Golden Showers' and the red 'Dance du Feu', all of which go on flowering throughout the summer.
Flowers Jun–Oct. Approx height and spread 2.5 × 2 m (8 × 6 ft).

Virginia creeper (*Parthenocissus* species) is worth growing for its superb autumn colour, and if you make a point of seeking out *Parthenocissus henryana*, you will also get the benefit of its beautiful, dark, velvety green leaves deeply veined with silver and pink in summer. It's not as vigorous as some of the other Virginia creepers, but quite vigorous enough to cover a garden wall or fence in a couple of years. Like all its relatives, it's a self-clinger.
Approx. height and spread after five years 2.5 × 1.5 m (8 × 5 ft); after ten years 5 × 3 m (16 × 10 ft).

SHRUBS

Japanese maples (*Acer palmatum* and *A. p* 'Dissectum') are among the most beautiful small foliage shrubs there are, with lovely leaves of bright green, in shades of red or purple, and even, in the case of one very recent introduction (*A. p.* 'Yuki-goma'), variegated green, cream and pink. *Acer palmatum*'s leaves are, as its name suggests, hand-shaped, while *A. p.* 'Dissectum' has deeply dissected, feathery leaves. Many varieties have very good autumn colour, and most form very small, umbrella-shaped trees with an attractive outline in the winter months. Apart from a lime-free soil, they need shelter from cold winds and late spring frosts. They also need dappled shade: strong midday sun can scorch the foliage and cause quite serious damage. They are ideal focal points in a border.
Approx. height and spread after five years 80 cm × 1 m ($2\frac{1}{2}$ × 3 ft); after ten years 1.2 × 1.5 m (4 × 5 ft).

Spotted laurel (*Aucuba japonica*), much loved by the Victorians but out of fashion for many years, will grow happily in practically any type of soil, including a limy one, and will also tolerate deep shade. Female forms will produce clusters of bright red berries in autumn and keep them throughout the winter, but only if there is a male form nearby. Look for 'Crotonifolia' (male, which has large leaves speckled with gold, and 'Variegata' (female), whose smaller leaves are splashed with gold and yellow over about half their area. It grows quite large but you can cut it back, so it's a good choice for the back of a border or very shady corner.
Approx. height and spread after five years 1.2 × 1.2 m (4 × 4 ft); after ten years 1.8 × 1.8 m ($5\frac{1}{2}$ × $5\frac{1}{2}$ ft).

Clematis 'Nelly Moser' does best in part-shade since too much sun causes the flower colour to fade.

Dogwood (*Cornus* species) is another excellent, accommodating shrub for small gardens since many varieties provide very attractive plain or variegated foliage in spring and summer, and vivid bark – scarlet or yellow – in the winter months. It will tolerate waterlogged soil and some lime, and though it does also grow in full sun, it will grow happily in shade. Good varieties to look out for include *Cornus alba* 'Elegantissima', which has beautiful pale green and white variegated foliage, and 'Spaethii' which has variegated gold and green leaves; both of these have brilliant red stems in winter. 'Westonbirt' is another attractive dogwood with fresh green foliage and the brightest red stems of all. *C. stolonifera* 'Flaviramea' has soft green foliage which turns yellow in autumn, revealing butter-yellow stems – a good contrast to the red-stemmed varieties. To get the best and brightest-coloured bark, you need to prune the stems hard back each spring which means that the shrub never grows bigger than the amount of growth it can make in one season. Approx. height and spread after five years (if unpruned) 2.5 × 3 m (8 × 10 ft); after ten years 2.5 × 4 m (8 × 13 ft).

False castor-oil plant (*Fatsia japonica*) is often thought of as a

The delicate foliage of the Japanese maple *Acer palmatum* 'Dissectum', seen here in a blaze of autumn colour, needs protection from direct sun; it is a superb feature shrub for a shady border.

houseplant, but in fact it is extremely hardy and thrives in deep to medium shade. It is what's known as an architectural shrub because of the bold, dramatic shape of its large, handsome, glossy, evergreen leaves. In spring it produces spikes of creamy-white flowers rather like golf balls, which eventually turn into clusters of black berries. Removing these will encourage the plant to produce larger leaves. There is a variegated version, but it is nothing like as hardy as its plain green cousin.

Approx. height and spread after five years 1 × 1 m (3 × 3 ft); after ten years 2 × 2 m (6 × 6 ft).

Garryea elliptica is an evergreen, grown mainly for its long, pale, grey-green catkins in winter. Some people feel that the rather dull green foliage during the rest of the year is too high a price to pay, but if you want to grow one, make sure it's 'James Roof', the catkins of which are extra long.

Approx. height and spread after five years 2.5 × 1.5 m (8 × 5 ft); after ten years 3.5 × 2.5 m (12 × 8 ft).

Chinese witch hazel (*Hamamelis mollis*) is grown for its sweetly scented, yellow, spider-like flowers which appear all up the bare stems in winter and early spring. They're followed by large, oval or even round leaves which have good autumn colour. The usual advice is to plant a scented winter flowerer like this one near a window or where you'll pass it frequently, but Rosemary Verey makes the point that it's usually too cold to have windows open in winter and prominent places you pass frequently deserve something that's more spectacular in spring and summer too. Perhaps the most beautiful form is *H. m.* 'Pallida' which has silvery-yellow flowers and attractive lustrous leaves, while *H.* × 'Jelena' and *H.* 'Ruby Glow', which have coppery-orange and coppery-red flowers respectively, are also worth considering.

Approx. height and spread after five years 1.5 × 2 m (5 × 6 ft); after ten years 3 × 4 m (10 × 13 ft).

Hydrangeas are among the most spectacular summer-flowering shrubs. There are many different sorts, of which the best known are the 'mop-head' varieties, with large, round heads of flowers, and the 'lace-caps' which have flatter flower heads. They're happy in medium shade and will grow on most moist soils, though the flower colour is affected by acidity or alkalinity – many forms are blue on acid soil and pink on limy soil. Look for *Hydrangea macrophylla* 'Hamburg' or 'Mme Emile Mouillière' (both 'mop-heads') and *H. m.* 'Mariesii', 'Blue Wave' or 'White Wave' which has white outer flowers and pink or blue central ones depending on the soil (all 'lace-caps'). One less common variety, well worth considering for deep shade, is the oak-leaved hydrangea (*H. quercifolia*), which has white flowers from midsummer through till autumn and fine orange-red autumn colour. It also tolerates dry soils.

Approx. height and spread after five years 1 × 1.2 m (3 × 4 ft); after ten years 2 × 2 m (6 × 6 ft).

Pachysandra teminalis, happiest on a neutral or acid soil, forms a carpet of serrated, diamond-shaped, light green leaves and spikes of small white flowers in mid-spring. It will thrive in deep shade, provided there is enough moisture. It can be a little invasive.

Approx. height and spread after five years 20 cm × 1 m (8 in × 3 ft); after ten years 30 cm × 1.5 m (1 × 5 ft).

Firethorn (*Pyracantha* species) is an ideal shrub for training against a shady wall. It has glossy, evergreen leaves, white flowers in early summer, and yellow, orange or red berries in autumn. Good varieties include *Pyracantha coccinea* 'Mojave', with orange-red berries; *P.* 'Orange Glow', with very dark foliage and orange berries; and *P.* 'Soleil d'Or', with mid-green leaves and deep yellow berries.

Flowers May–Jun. Approx. height and spread after five years 2 × 1.2 m (6 × 4 ft); after ten years 3.5 × 2 m (12 × 6 ft).

Willow (*Salix* species) is another large family with many members worth considering for moist shade. Of the smaller-growing ones *Salix × boydii*, which has round, green leaves covered with woolly down when young, forms a gnarled-looking bush which never reaches more than 50×70 cm ($1\frac{1}{2} \times 2\frac{1}{2}$ ft) – ideal for the front of a border or even for a trough. Eventually reaching about twice the size of *S. × boydii* but even more attractive is the woolly willow (*S. lanata*), with its grey leaves and small, yellowish-grey catkins which appear at the same time as the new leaves. *S. hastata* 'Wehrhahnii' has masses of large, silvery-white catkins on dark purplish stems and eventually forms a rounded, spreading bush approximately 1.2×1.2 m (4×4 ft).

Of the medium-sized willows, the coyote willow (*S. exigua*) is a superb background shrub with very fine, long, silky, silver leaves, as well as pale yellow catkins in spring. It will reach 3–4 m (10–13 ft) in ten years, but produces more attractive foliage if it's pruned hard back every three or four years.

Golden elder (*Sambucus nigra* 'Aurea') adds a splash of brightness to a shady border. It produces its brightest-coloured foliage on new wood, so it's best pruned back hard each spring, which also limits its size to the amount of growth it can make in one season. Its showier relative, the cut-leaved golden elder (*Sambucus racemosa* 'Plumosa Aurea'), which has very deeply cut, divided foliage, needs more light, though it will thrive in dappled shade.
Approx. height and spread after five years (unpruned) 3×2 m (10×6 ft); after ten years 4×3.5 m (13×12 ft).

Christmas box (*Sarcococca humilis*) is a dwarf, evergreen, thicket-forming shrub that has narrow, pointed, glossy green leaves and sweetly scented, small white flowers as early as February. It needs a rich soil, but will tolerate some alkalinity, and will grow in deep shade though not quite as well as it does with a little more light.
Approx. height and spread after five years 25×30 cm (10×12 in); after ten years 50×40 cm (18×16 in).

Skimmia is another invaluable small evergreen shrub, provided it gets the right soil conditions – it won't tolerate any alkalinity and dislikes extremes of waterlogging and drought. It has shiny aromatic leaves, scented white flowers in late spring, and clusters of shiny red or white berries in autumn. To be sure of berries you need to plant at least one male with any number of females. Good varieties include *Skimmia japonica* 'Nymans' or 'Foremanii' (both female) and *S. j.* 'Rubella', a male form which has short, fat pokers of deep red buds which open to blush-white, sweetly scented flowers.
Approx. height and spread after five years 40×40 cm (16×16 in); after ten years 60×60 cm (2×2 ft).

54. *Rodgersia*
    podophylla

3. *Hedera helix*
   'Goldheart'

19. *Photinia × f*
    'Red Robin'

18. *Weigela florida*
    'Variegata'

16. *Berberis thunbergii*
    'Aurea'

52. Bowles' golden
    grass

55. *Geranium nodosum*

53. *Viola labradorica*

2. *Lonicera*
   tellmanniana

50. *Brunnera*
    macrophylla

47. *Hosta* 'Honeybells'

1. *Hydrangea petiolaris*

12. *Prunus* 'Pink Shell'

46. *Rheum*
    'Ace of
    Hearts'

49. *Hosta fortunei*
    'Aurea'

1. *Heuchera* 'Palace
Purple'

48. *Hosta* 'Buckshaw
Blue'

20. *Sopraea × bumalda*
'Goldflame'

15. *Eleagnus*
pungens
'Maculata'

Snowberry (*Symphoricarpos* species) is another shrub grown primarily for its berries – not only white, but many shades of pink as well. Some forms produce lots of suckers which can be a nuisance, so make sure you go for a non-suckering variety like *S.* × *doorenbosii* 'Magic Berry', with small mauve-carmine berries, or *S.* × *d.* 'Mother of Pearl', which is a semi-weeping form with large, white, pink-tinged berries.

Approx. height and spread after five years 1.5 × 1 m (5 × 3 ft); after ten years 2.5 × 2 m (8 × 6 ft).

Viburnum is another family with a member to suit practically every garden situation.

Viburnum davidii, which forms an attractive, low, spreading, evergreen shrub, has large, leathery, dark green, glossy leaves. The white flowers in June are followed by striking turquoise fruits, provided there is a male plant around to pollinate the female. It's not always easy to be sure you've got bushes of both sexes, but if you have enough room, plant at least three and so increase the odds!

Approx. height and spread after five years 80 × 80 cm ($2\frac{1}{2}$ × $2\frac{1}{2}$ ft); after ten years 1.2 × 1.2 m (4 × 4 ft).

The **guelder rose** (*Viburnum opulus*) is even more accommodating – it will grow in waterlogged or dry soil and is tolerant of acidity and alkalinity. *Viburnum opulus* 'Sterile', the snowball shrub, produces, as its common name suggests, white snowball-like flowerheads in May or June. As its botanical name indicates, it doesn't bear any berries, whereas *V. o.* 'Notcutt's Variety' produces both white 'lace-cap' flowers not unlike those of the hydrangea and large clusters of transluscent red berries in autumn. It's also worth thinking about the much smaller *V. o.* 'Compactum', which has white lace-cap flowers and red fruits but reaches only half the size of the other two. A viburnum that divides opinion sharply is *V. rhytidophyllum*, which makes a large shrub with huge, leathery, deeply veined leaves that have grey-brown, felty undersides which droop in cold weather. It has heads of buff white flowers, then red berries which eventually turn black. Some people think it's dull, others regard it as a striking, architectural shrub – an acquired taste perhaps, but good in a shady corner. It can grow quite a lot bigger than the other viburnums mentioned here.

Approx. height and spread after five years 1.5 × 1.5 m (5 × 5 ft); after ten years 3 × 3 m (10 × 10 ft).

HERBACEOUS PLANTS

Monkshood (*Aconitum* species), with its tall spikes of hooded, dark blue flowers and glossy, deeply divided leaves, is a good choice for

the back of a partially shaded border, though since it is poisonous in all its parts it is best avoided if you have small children. Good varieties include: *Aconitum napellus* 'Bressingham Spire', *A. carmichaelii* 'Arendsii' (both deep blue) or the shorter-growing, creamy-yellow-flowered *A. orientale*.
Flowers Jul–Aug. Approx. height and spread after five years 1 m × 40 cm (3 ft × 16 in).

Lady's mantle (*Alchemilla mollis*) is a star among herbaceous plants. Its fresh green leaves look like carefully folded fans as they open, and it carries sprays of tiny yellow-green flowers for months on end. It will grow practically anywhere – in sun or shade, in soil that is damp or dry, acid or alkaline. It seeds itself with alacrity in the crevices of paving, in walls and steps, but usually looks so good that you just leave it there.
Flowers Jun–Aug. Approx. height and spread 50 × 30 cm ($1\frac{1}{2}$ × 1 ft).

Japanese anemones (*Anemone × hybrida*) provide late summer-early autumn colour with their masses of tall pink or white flowering stems. Good varieties to look out for include *Anemone × hybrida* 'Queen Charlotte', with semi-double, rich pink flowers with gold stamens, and *A. × hybrida* 'Alba' or the tall *A. × hybrida* 'Honorine Jobert', both with large white flowers.
Flowers Aug–Oct. Approx. height and spread 50–100 × 35 cm ($1\frac{1}{2}$–3 ft × 15 in).

Columbines (*Aquilegia* species) are beautiful cottage-garden plants with flowers in a whole range of colours from white and blue through pink, red and yellow. Many of the widely available hybrids like 'McKana' or 'Mrs Scott Elliott' have bi-colour flowers – white and red, pink and yellow, and so on. Their foliage, a little like that of the maidenhair fern, is also attractive. They like dappled shade under trees or shrubs.
Flowers May–Aug. Approx. height and spread 60 × 40 cm (2 ft × 16 in).

Astilbes, which tolerate really damp soil, are usually grown for their elegant plumes of tiny flowers in shades of pink, red and white, but their ferny foliage is equally attractive. Good forms of the tall-growing *Astilbe × arendsii* include the red 'Fanal' and the rose-pink *A. × a.* 'Federsee', while for the front of the border the much smaller varieties, *A. chinensis* 'Pumila', which has mauve-pink flowers, and *A. simplicifolia* 'Bronze Elegance', which has creamy salmon-pink flowers and lovely bronze-tinged foliage, would be excellent choices.
Flowers Jun–Aug. Approx. height and spread 120 × 50 cm (4 × $1\frac{1}{2}$ ft); dwarf varieties 30 × 50 cm (1 × $1\frac{1}{2}$ ft).

Masterwort (*Astrantia major*) makes you wonder how such a

54. *Rodgersia
podophylla*

3. *Hedera helix*
'Goldheart'

18. *Weigela florida*
'Variegata'

19. *Photinia ×
frazerii*
'Red Robin'

52. Bowles'
golden grass

16. *Berberis
thunbergii*
'Aurea'

55. *Geranium
nodosum*

53. *Viola
labradorica*

2. *Lonicera tellmanniana*

50. *Brunnera macrophylla*

1. *Hydrangea petiolaris*

12. *Prunus* 'Pink Shell'

46. *Rheum* 'Ace of Hearts'

49. *Hosta fortunei* 'Aurea'

48. *Hosta* 'Buckshaw Blue'

20. *Spiraea* × *bumalda* 'Goldflame'

15. *Eleagnus pungens* 'Maculata'

51. *Heuchera* 'Palace Purple'

47. *Hosta* 'Honeybells'

beautiful plant got such an ugly common name! Its pink, cream and green flowers with their pin-cushion centres really are exquisite, like miniature Victorian posies. There is a form of *Astrantia major* – 'Sunningdale Variegated' – whose foliage is marked with a lighter green fading to cream, to give interest in the border after the flowers have faded.

Flowers Jun–Sept. Approx. height and spread 60 × 40 cm (2 ft × 16 in).

Elephant's ears (*Bergenia* species) has very attractive, large, rounded, evergreen leaves, some of which take on a bronze or red tint in winter. They also have spikes of white, pink or red flowers in spring and summer. Good varieties to look out for include *Bergenia cordifolia* 'Purpurea' which has large, wavy, round leaves that turn a purplish-red in winter and magenta flowers on and off throughout the summer; *B.* 'Abendglut' with neat, crinkle-edged leaves, good autumn colour and vivid rose-red flowers; and *B.* 'Ballawley', the largest of all, with good autumn colour and rose-red flowers in spring, and occasionally a few in autumn.

Flowers Mar onwards according to variety. Approx. height and spread 30–60 cm × 30–60 cm (15 in–2 ft × 15 in–2 ft).

Marsh marigold (*Caltha palustris*), as the name suggests, likes it really damp and will even grow in shallow water. It has shiny, round leaves and bright, buttercup-yellow flowers in spring. The double-flowered variety, *Caltha palustris* 'Plena', is even more attractive, while the white-flowered variety *C. p.* 'Alba' has simple white flowers with bright gold stamens and sometimes produces a second crop in autumn (this one won't grow in water).

Flowers Mar–May. Approx. height and spread 20 × 35 cm (8 × 13 in).

Bugbane (*Cimicifuga* species) is another plant a thousand times more attractive than its name. It has lovely ferny foliage and in autumn produces clusters of 'bottle brush' flowers on tall stems, which turn into attractive lime-green seed heads – a good plant for the back of the border. Look for *Cimicifuga simplex* 'White Pearl'.

Flowers Aug–Oct. Approx. height and spread 130 × 70 cm ($4\frac{1}{2}$ ft × 28 in).

Bleeding heart (*Dicentra spectabilis*) is a beautiful, late spring-early summer flowering plant, with graceful arching stems of small flowers like deep pink hearts with a white teardrop underneath. It also has attractive ferny foliage which dies down in midsummer, so don't panic and think you've somehow managed to kill it off! There is also a very beautiful white version, *Dicentra spectabilis* 'Alba'.

Flowers May–Jun. Approx. height and spread 60 × 50 cm ($2 \times 1\frac{1}{2}$ ft).

Christmas rose (*Helleborus niger*) and Lenten rose (*Helleborus orientalis*) are members of a family no shady garden should be without. The Christmas rose (more usually in flower in January than at Christmas, incidentally) has leathery, evergreen leaves, and large, waxy, white flowers with gold stamens that last for weeks. The Lenten rose, which flowers in late winter, has similar-shaped flowers but in a whole range of colours from white and green through mauve-pinks to purple. It's a slightly larger plant than the Christmas rose and both of them are happy in limy soil.

Flowers: Jan–Mar – Christmas rose; Feb–Apr – Lenten rose. Approx. height and spread 30×40 cm (12×16 in) – Christmas rose; 50×50 cm ($1\frac{1}{2} \times 1\frac{1}{2}$ ft) – Lenten rose.

Coral flower (*Heuchera sanguinea*) makes good weed-suppressing clumps of scalloped evergreen leaves in dappled shade and rich soil and produces tall, thin stems of tiny red or pink flowers. An interesting variety with mounds of bronzy, wine-coloured foliage and sprays of tiny, white flowers is *Heuchera sanguinea* 'Palace Purple' – a good contrast with a silvery-leafed ground-cover plant like dead nettle (*Lamium* species).

Flowers Apr–Jun. Approx. height and spread 60×50 cm ($2 \times 1\frac{1}{2}$ ft).

Plantain lily (*Hosta* species) is an outstanding foliage plant and a reason all on its own for having a shady area in your garden. There are many different ones to choose from, some with very small leaves, like *Hosta minor*, and some with huge leaves like *H. sieboldiana* 'Elegans' which has blue-green, deeply ribbed leaves almost 30 cm (1 ft) wide. There are gold-leafed varieties, like *H. fortunei* 'Aurea', and others in many shades of green and blue as well as the variegated forms like *H.* 'Thomas Hogg', whose elegant, pointed leaves have creamy margins. Hostas also flower, producing spikes of either mauve or white flowers, and have good autumn colour before the leaves finally rot away. The only snag with hostas is that slugs and snails love them almost as much as discerning gardeners, and can reduce a large leaf to something resembling a collander overnight. Some form of anti-slug precaution is essential.

Flowers Jul–Aug. Approx. height and spread (of foliage) 30–60 cm × 30 cm–1 m (1–2 ft × 1–3 ft).

Dead nettle (*Lamium maculatum*) is a marvellous ground-cover plant for shade, spreading quickly and covering a large area with attractive, variegated foliage, creating areas of light among the shade. *Lamium maculatum* 'Beacon Silver', *L. m.* 'White Nancy' and *L. m.* 'Shell-Pink' all have silver-variegated leaves and produce clear pink, ivory white and shell-pink flowers respectively. After the flowers have faded, it's worth trimming the plant with shears to remove the dead flower heads and any upward-growing leafy shoots to keep it close to the ground.

Flowers May–Jul. Approx. height and spread 20×50 cm (8×18 in).

Columbines (*Aquilegia*), in a range of delicate colours, thrive in part-shade.

Omphalodes cappodocica is a very useful ground-cover plant for growing under acid-loving shrubs since it does best in peaty soil and part-shade, but it will still give a good show in neutral soil. Although its oval, slightly crinkled leaves are not spectacular, it produces sprays of the most vivid gentian-blue flowers, not unlike those of forget-me-nots but larger, for weeks on end.

Flowers Apr–May. Approx. height and spread 20 × 40 cm (8 × 16 in).

Solomon's seal (*Polygonatum × hybridum*) is one of those woodland plants with a quiet beauty. It has elegant arching stems with long, fresh green leaves all the way up, from which dangle small, white flowers rather like miniature white pears with a green base. There is a variegated form, *P. multiflorum* 'Variegatum', with leaves boldly striped in creamy white. As with hostas, slugs find the foliage irresistible.

Flowers May–Jun. Approx. height and spread 80 × 40 cm ($2\frac{1}{2}$ ft × 16 in).

Knotweed (*Polygonum* species) is another large family, some of whose members are true garden thugs, smothering everything in sight and to be avoided, while others are better-behaved and make good, weed-suppressing clumps. They carry masses of pink or red flowers, rather like fluffy pokers, in summer and autumn. A good variety to look out for is the low-growing *Polygonum affine* 'Dimity', whose pink flowers darken to a rusty red with age and whose fresh green foliage turns russet brown in winter and stays on the plant until new growth appears in spring. If it does get over-ambitious, simply chop it back with a spade. The much taller *P. bistorta* 'Superbum' is also a good variety with much larger, dock-like, light green leaves and large, clear pink flowers in early summer and sometimes again in early autumn.

Flowers Jul–Sept. – *P. affine*; May and Sept – *P. bistorta*. Approx. height and spread 23 × 50 cm (9 × 18 in) – *P. affine*; 90 × 70 cm (3 ft × 2 ft 3 in) – *P. bistorta*.

Primulas are another large family with members for almost every garden situation. The lovely candelabra primulas (so called because their flowers are arranged in whorls up their stems), *Primula japonica* and *P. beesiana,* and the drumstick primula (*P. denticulata*) all need a moist neutral or acid soil to do well. The auricula primulas with their lovely, bi-coloured flowers – rich reds, blues with gold markings – are also supposed to dislike lime, but they grow beautifully in Rosemary Verey's chalky soil. The common primrose (*P. vulgaris*) will grow almost anywhere as long as the soil is rich and moist.
Flowers Mar–Jul. Approx. height and spread 30–60 × 30 cm (1–2 × 1 ft).

Lungwort (*Pulmonaria* species) is an excellent ground-cover plant for moist shade. It bears sprays of small pink, white or blue flowers in spring, followed by clumps of weed-smothering, attractive leaves – spotted or silver-frosted. Good varieties to look out for include *Pulmonaria officinalis* 'Cambridge Blue', which has heart-shaped, spotted leaves and masses of blue flowers opening from pink buds, giving it a bi-colour effect; *P. saccharata* 'Sissinghurst White', which has much larger leaves marbled with silver and large, white flowers; and *P. s.* 'Highdown', which has rich blue flowers.
Flowers Mar–May. Approx. height and spread 30 × 30 cm (1 × 1 ft).

Above: Christmas rose (*Helleborus niger*).

Left: Bleeding heart (*Dicentra spectabilis*).

Wake robin (*Trillium grandiflorum*) is a superb woodland plant, not as widely known as it deserves to be. In a moist acid or neutral soil (any lime will kill it), it produces clusters of three shiny mid-green leaves, above which appear its pure white, three-petalled flowers.
Flowers Mar–May. Approx. height and spread 40 × 30 cm (16 × 12 in).

Viola labradorica is an excellent ground-cover plant that seeds itself so freely when it's established that it could almost be a nuisance if it weren't so attractive! It has small, round, green leaves flushed with purple, while its flowers, produced in spring, are small mauve violets, whose colour is exactly the right tone for the leaves.
Flowers Mar–May. Approx. height and spread 10–15 × 30 cm (4–6 × 12 in).

ANNUALS
While the vast majority of annuals really need a sunny position, there are a few which will do well in shade and they are such excellent plants that their quality almost compensates for the very limited choice.

Fibrous-rooted begonia (*Begonia semperflorens*), with flowers in white, red and pink and foliage that's green or wine red, will do very well in shade.
Flowers Jun–Oct. Approx. height and spread 15–25 × 25 cm (6–10 × 10 in).

Busy Lizzie (*Impatiens* species) is a superb choice for a shady border because it will go on flowering prolifically from June until the first frosts. It comes in a whole range of colours, from pure white through many shades of pink and salmon to orange, red and even violet, though in a shady spot paler colours – white, very pale pink or mauve – really do seem to gleam while brighter ones rather lose their impact. Again, it's a matter of personal taste, but a clump, all the same colour, looks more effective than mixed colours. Unfortunately, many garden centres or even street markets sell annuals like busy Lizzie in mixed colours, so it's worth hunting out those which offer trays of a single colour.
Flowers Jun–Nov. Approx. height and spread 20–30 × 20 cm (8–12 × 8 in).

Lobelia is an excellent space filler at the front of a border. Look for 'Crystal Palace', which has intense blue flowers set off to perfection by its bronzy foliage; 'Mrs Clibran', deep blue with a white eye; and 'White Lady', which sometimes produces a few pale blue flowers along with the white. For hanging baskets and containers, try a trailing variety like 'Blue Cascade' or 'Sapphire' whose intense blue flowers have a white eye.
Flowers Jun–Sept. Approx. height and spread 15 × 15 cm (6 × 6 in).

Monkey flower (*Mimulus* species) produces masses of small, trumpet-shaped flowers in a range of brilliant colours – red, orange, yellow, burgundy, pink and white – and many of them are spotted or blotched with a contrasting colour. Once the first flush of flowers is over, trim the plants back to encourage more flowers.
Flowers Jun–Sept. Approx. height and spread 20 × 20 cm (8 × 8 in).

Baby blue eyes (*Nemophila insignis*) is a very pretty, front-of-the-border plant with sky-blue, cup-shaped flowers with white centres carried above slightly trailing, ferny foliage. It's a hardy annual, so it can be sown straight into the ground where you want it to flower.
Flowers Jun–Sept. Approx. height and spread 15 × 15 (6 × 6 in).

Heartsease (*Viola tricolor*), our native pansy, has really delightful small flowers in yellow, violet and mauve – usually all three together. It's happy in dappled shade and in most soil types including sand. It is actually a very short-lived perennial but is best treated as an annual. Once it's established, it will seed itself and flower from May onwards.
Flowers May–Oct. Approx. height and spread 10–20 × 10 cm (4–8 × 4 in).

BULBS

Many flowering bulbs thrive in woodland conditions during spring and autumn when the trees under which they grow are bare of leaves and so allow a reasonable amount of light and moisture through. Although it's tempting to fill the spaces *between* clumps of herbaceous plants with bulbs, it's probably better to plant your bulbs *in among* individual clumps. For one thing, as mentioned earlier, the foliage of the herbaceous plants will disguise the bulbs' foliage once flowering is over – always a problem, since you have to leave it to die down naturally. For another, you'll probably want to fill the gaps with annuals for some summer colour, and that's much more difficult if those gaps are already filled with bulbs.

Arum italicum 'Pictum' is an exotic-looking plant which produces heads of poisonous, bright orange berries like drumsticks in late summer followed by the leaves, which are spear-shaped, glossy dark green, strikingly marked with grey and cream, and which keep appearing until the spring.
Flowers (insignificant) Apr–May. Approx. height and spread 30–45 × 30 cm (12–18 × 12 in). Plant 30 cm (12 in) apart.

Glory of the snow (*Chionodoxa luciliae*) had very pretty blue-lilac flowers with a white eye. If left undisturbed, they will seed themselves.
Flowers Mar–Apr. Approx. height 5 cm (2 in). Plant 8–10 cm (3–4 in) apart.

Above: Subtle winter colour beneath a tree from the pale green *Helleborus corsicus*, snowdrops and the variegated leaves of *Arum italicum* 'Pictum'.

Above right: *Primula pulverulenta* thrives in damp shade.

Cyclamen hederifolium produces masses of deep pink or white flowers which are thumbnail-sized versions of the pot plants we buy. The beautiful, ivy-shaped leaves, which are marbled with silver, follow the flowers. Cyclamen will tolerate some degree of alkalinity, but a soil just either side of neutral suits them best.
Flowers Aug–Nov. Approx. height 3 cm (1 in). Plant 8–10 cm (3–4 in) apart.

Winter aconite (*Eranthis hyemalis*) with its bright yellow, buttercup-like flowers set on a ruff of dark green leaves, is one of the first bulbs to appear after Christmas. It's happy in moist soils – acid or alkaline – and in shade. The tubers are usually sold dry, and can become very hard, so soak them overnight in water before planting or, if possible, put them in a seed tray of moist peat for a couple of weeks.
Flowers Jan–Mar. Approx. height 3–5 cm (1–2 in). Plant 5–8 cm (2–3 in) apart.

Dog's-tooth violet (*Erythronium dens-canis*) has beautiful, delicate, nodding flowers in shades of white, pink, lilac and carmine, and attractive mottled leaves. Good varieties to look for include *Erythronium dens-canis* 'White Splendour', 'Rose Beauty' and 'Lilac Wonder'. Again, the tubers dislike drying out, so buy them from a reputable supplier and plant them as soon as you receive them.
Flowers Mar–Apr. Approx. height 10–15 cm (4–6 in). Plant 15–20 cm (6–8 in) apart.

Snowdrops (*Galanthus nivalis*) are among the earliest of the spring-flowering bulbs and their pure white flowers show up very well in shade. They tolerate most types of soil, though in a sandy soil you need to dig in plenty of moisture-retaining organic matter before planting. There are lots of different varieties – some with double flowers, like *Galanthus nivalis* 'Flore Pleno', and some with beautiful green markings on the petals, like *G. n.* 'Viridapicis' – and they are best planted 'in the green', just after they have flowered. Although you can also buy them as dried bulbs in autumn, they may take a couple of years to settle down and start growing well.
Flowers Jan–Mar. Approx. height 5 cm (2 in). Plant 5–8 cm (2–3 in) apart.

Spring snowflakes (*Leocojum vernum*) are related to snowdrops but have longer stems and more rounded, white, scented flowers.
Flowers Mar–May. Approx. height 8 cm (3 in). Plant 15–20 cm (6–8 in) apart.

Grape hyacinths (*Muscari armeniacum*), with their dense spikes of vivid blue flowers, are widely grown, though this particular variety, which will tolerate shade, is taller and has paler blue flowers than the most commonly grown variety, *Muscari botryoides*.
Flowers Apr–May. Approx. height 10–15 cm (4–6 in). Plant 10–15 cm (4–6 in) apart.

Busy Lizzie (*Impatiens*), in a wide range of colours, is the ideal annual for a shady border.

Daffodils (*Narcissus cyclamineus*) will cope with shady conditions, provided they are the smaller species daffodils, not the huge golden garden hybrids. After all, the latter didn't exist when the daffodils that made such a deep impression on W. Wordsworth were fluttering and dancing 'beside the lake, beneath the trees'. Look for *Narcissus cyclamineus* 'February Gold'; the smaller 'Tête à Tête', with two or three flowers on each stem which often start opening as soon as the stem has emerged from the ground; or the lovely white 'Jenny'. Like all the members of this family they need well-drained but moisture-retentive soil, and if you feed them after they've flowered with bone meal or a general-purpose fertiliser such as Growmore, they will go on flowering for many years.

Flowers Feb–Apr. Approx. height 15–30 cm (6–12 in). Plant 20–30 cm (8–12 in) apart.

Dry Shade

As already explained, dry shade is one of the most difficult garden situations to fill with suitable plants, but by no means impossible. You can help a lot by improving the soil as much as you are able with moisture-retentive organic matter before you plant, and by mulching the border with a good thick layer of more of the same in the autumn and again in spring. If part of the problem is caused by a dense canopy of overhanging branches, removing a few selectively will improve matters. But do make sure, before you get busy with the saw, that the tree isn't covered by any kind of preservation order. If it is, you'll have to get permission before you do any work on it.

CLIMBERS

Ivy (*Hedera helix* or *H. colchica*), the climbing hydrangea (*Hydrangea petiolaris*) and Virginia creeper (*Parthenocissus* species) will all tolerate dry shade. (See pages 58 and 59.)

SHRUBS

Snowy mespilus (*Amelanchier lamarckii*) is a shrub (or small tree) with a long season of interest – from its clouds of small, white flowers along with new bronzy foliage in spring to its stunning autumn colour. It is supposed to grow really successfully only on acid soils, but it sometimes copes well enough with neutral and even chalky soils (if they are moist) to make it worth a try.

Approx. height and spread after five years 4 × 3 m (13 × 10 ft); after ten years 7.5 × 6 m (25 × 20 ft).

Barberry (*Berberis* species) is a family of tough, accommodating shrubs, some of which will put on a reasonable show in dry shade. They include the evergreens *Berberis darwinii*, which has small, jagged, evergreen leaves and clusters of bright orange flowers in spring, and *B. stenophylla*, which has long, thin leaves, olive on top, silver underneath, and double, yellow flowers hanging along its curving branches in spring. Among the deciduous barberries, the green- and gold-leafed varieties of *B. thunbergii* will tolerate shade, though the many purple-, red- and pink-leafed ones need sun to maintain their colour.

Approx. height and spread after five years 1.5 × 1.5 m (5 × 5 ft); after ten years 2.2 × 2 m (7 × 6 ft).

Spindle (*Euonymus fortunei*) is a very versatile evergreen shrub that will either climb up a shady wall, if pointed in the right direction, or spread along the ground. There are several good variegated forms: among the green-and-golds look for *Euonymus fortunei* 'Emerald and Gold' and 'Gold Tip'; and among the quieter cream-and-greens *E. f.* 'Emerald Gaity' and, for climbing, *E. f.* 'Variegatus', both of whose leaves are flushed pink in very cold weather.

Approx. height and spread after five years 60 cm × 1 m (2 × 3 ft); after ten years 60 cm × 2 m (2 × 6 ft); climbing – after ten years 4 × 4 m (13 × 13 ft).

Holly (*Ilex aquifolium*), like its traditional partner ivy, will put up with dry shade and the variegated forms will brighten a dark corner. Both *Ilex* 'Silver Queen', with white markings, and *I.* 'Golden King', with gold variegations, are good varieties. To confuse matters, 'Silver Queen' is a male form (no berries) while 'Golden King' is female (bearing berries provided there is a male somewhere in the area)! Of the plain green hollies *I.* 'J. C. van Tol' has a lot to offer – almost spineless, it bears glossy green leaves and regular crops of red berries.

Approx. height and spread after five years 2 × 1.5 m (6 × 5 ft); after ten years 4 × 2.5 m (13 × 8 ft).

Winter-flowering jasmine (*Jasminum nudiflorum*) is marvellous value in a small garden and really lights up a north wall. In some years it will start producing its starry yellow flowers on bare green stems as early as November and carries on till March. It's a wall shrub rather than a climber and so will need some support, but it's at its best trailing downwards, so tie it back near the top of the wall or fence and allow it to spill over the twine.

Approx. height and spread after five years 1.5 × 1.5 m (5 × 5 ft); after ten years 2 × 2 m (6 × 6 ft).

Oregon grape (*Mahonia aquifolium*) is a superb shrub for dry shade. It has long, jagged, evergreen leaves, sprays of scented, yellow flowers in early spring, and in autumn the leaves turn a purplish-red. It can get a little straggly, particularly in deep shade,

2. *Helleborus foetidus* × 3

1. *Aucuba japonica* 'Variegata'

30. *Hydrangea petiolaris*

27. *Viburnum opulus*

26. *Ribes sanguineum*

22. *Euonymus fortunei* 'Emerald 'n' gold'

21. *Anemone japo* (white) × 3

12. *Cyclamen hederifolium*

8. Bowles' golden grass × 3

7. *Impatiens walleriana* × 6

20. *Brunnera macropylla*

9. *Galanthus nivalis* × 10

6. *Dicentra eximia* × 3

4. *Pulmonaria saccharata* 'Sissinghurst' × 3

3. *Bergenia* × 3

5. *Geranium macrorrhizum* × 3

10. *Viola labradorica* × 3

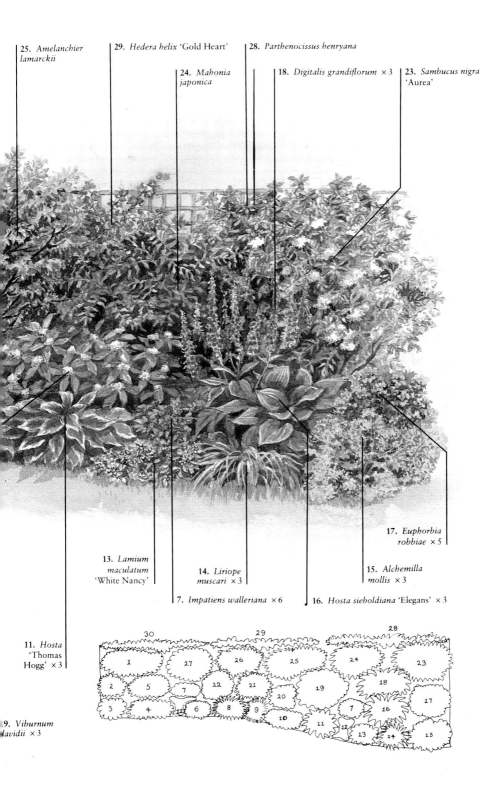

25. *Amelanchier lamarckii*

29. *Hedera helix* 'Gold Heart'

28. *Parthenocissus henryana*

24. *Mahonia japonica*

18. *Digitalis grandiflorum* × 3

23. *Sambucus nigra* 'Aurea'

17. *Euphorbia robbiae* × 5

13. *Lamium maculatum* 'White Nancy'

14. *Liriope muscari* × 3

15. *Alchemilla mollis* × 3

7. *Impatiens walleriana* × 6

16. *Hosta sieboldiana* 'Elegans' × 3

11. *Hosta* 'Thomas Hogg' × 3

9. *Viburnum davidii* × 3

but if you cut back the old, woody growth to ground level every three or four years, it will produce new growth very quickly. *Mahonia japonica* has foliage that is deep green on acid soil and is tinged with red on a limy soil. It also has very fragrant yellow flowers which sometimes appear before Christmas. Look out for the hybrid M. 'Charity', which is one of the best – it is often labelled as a hybrid of M. *japonica* but is, in fact, a hybrid of M. *bealei*.

Approx. height and spread of M. *aquifolium* after five years 80 cm × 1 m ($2\frac{1}{2}$ × 3 ft); after ten years 1 × 2 m (3 × 6 ft); of M. *japonica* after five years 1.5 × 1.8 m (5 × $5\frac{1}{2}$ ft); after ten years 2.5 × 2.8 m (8 × 9 ft).

Cherry laurel (*Prunus laurocerasus* 'Otto Luyken') is a useful evergreen that will tolerate anything except extremely dry and/or extremely limy soil. It has glossy foliage and, in spring, candles of small, creamy white flowers. You may see it planted in public places where, quite often, the young shrubs are placed only 50 cm (18 in) apart. In fact, as the specimen in Rosemary Verey's garden makes clear, it will grow to 2 m (6 ft) across in ten years.

Approx. height and spread after five years 1 × 1 m (3 × 3 ft); after ten years 1.5 × 2 m (5 × 6 ft).

Flowering currant (*Ribes sanguineum* 'Pulborough Scarlet'), with its rose-red flowers in April or early May, does remarkably well in dry shade, as it does also in heavy clay. It reaches its final height very fast and is a useful shrub for achieving a quick effect.

Approx. height and spread after five years 1.5 × 1 m (5 × 3 ft); after ten years 2 × 2 m (6 × 6 ft).

Stag's horn sumach (*Rhus typhina*) seems a very exotic shrub to be growing in such difficult conditions. It has beautiful, fern-like foliage which turns scarlet in autumn, and in winter the bare tree, with the branching form that gives it its common name, is covered in reddish-brown, furry bark. It also has large, velvety, brown cones in autumn.

Approx. height and spread after five years 2 × 2 m (6 × 6 ft); after ten years 4 × 4 m (13 × 13 ft).

Golden elder (*Sambucus nigra* 'Aurea') will also tolerate dry shade, though it will lose some of its golden colour, becoming more golden-green. (See page 63.)

Skimmia will tolerate dry, but not extremely dry, conditions. (See page 63.)

Guelder rose (*Viburnum opulus*) will tolerate dry shade. (See page 66.)

Lesser periwinkle (*Vinca minor*) is a trailing, ground-covering, evergreen shrub which will tolerate deep shade and dry soil. It's more attractive and better suited to small gardens than the ordinary periwinkle (*Vinca major*). It flowers from April to June and among the best varieties are *Vinca minor* 'Bowles' Variety', which has large, light blue flowers, and 'Gertrude Jekyll', which has small, pure white flowers.

Approx. height and spread after five years 15 × 40 cm (6 × 16 in); after ten years 15 × 60 cm (6 in × 2 ft).

HERBACEOUS PLANTS

Bugle (*Ajuga reptans*), with short spikes on intense blue flowers in early summer, is a good carpeter. There are some lovely variegated kinds, though the green and pale buff 'Variegata' does better in deep shade than the dark metallic purple 'Atropurpurea' and the mottled wine-red 'Burgundy Glow'. They don't form such a dense carpet as they would in a moist soil, but they do well enough.

Flowers May–Jul. Approx. height and spread 15 cm × 1 m (6 in × 3 ft).

Lady's mantle (*Alchemilla mollis*) will also do well enough in dry shade. (See page 67.)

Elephant's ears (*Bergenia* species) won't flower as prolifically in dry shade as it will in moister conditions, but its large, thick, leathery leaves are well worth having. (See page 70.)

Siberian bugloss (*Brunnera macrophylla*), a perennial relation of the forget-me-not, has sprays of similar bright blue flowers in spring. It also bears large, heart-shaped leaves, though these won't be as big or as numerous as they would be in a moister soil.

Flowers Apr–May. Approx. height and spread 45 × 45 cm (18 × 18 in).

Eastern bleeding heart (*Dicentra eximia*) is a much bushier plant with more feathery foliage than its native cousin, though its pink flowers, borne intermittently throughout the summer after the first main flush in late spring, are more tubular than heart-shaped. Bleeding heart (*Dicentra spectabilis*) will tolerate dry shade to a degree, but *D. eximia* tolerates it better.

Flowers May–Oct. Approx. height and spread 30 × 50 cm (12 × 18 in).

Foxglove (*Digitalis* species) will do well in most soils, given some shade. Our native foxglove, *Digitalis purpurea*, is, strictly speaking, a bienniel (growing one year, flowering the next, then dying), but it may survive a year or two longer. It usually seeds itself pretty well, so continuity is not a problem. There are perennial foxgloves, like *D. grandiflora*, which has pale yellow flowers, and *D. ferruginea*, which has very unusual coppery-yellow flowers veined with brown.

Flowers Jun–Aug. Approx. height and spread 90 × 30 cm (3 × 1 ft).

Winter-flowering
Mahonia 'Charity'.

Barrenwort (*Epimedium* species) does best of all where there is some moisture in the soil, but even in dry shade it gives a good enough account of itself to be worth trying.
Flowers Apr–Jun. Approx. height and spread 30 × 30 cm (1 × 1 ft).

Spurge (*Euphorbia* species) is another large family with members for all situations. For dry shade the best is *Euphorbia robbiae*, which has tall rosettes of leathery, dark green leaves topped all summer long with yellow-green flowers which take on bronze tints in autumn.
Flowers Apr–Jun. Approx. height and spread 60 × 60 cm + (2 × 2 ft +).

Cranesbill (*Geranium* species) does sterling work in dry shade, particularly the *Geranium macrorrhizum* varieties. These have lovely, aromatic, semi-evergreen leaves, which sometimes turn red in autumn, and sprays of flowers in white or pink. Look for G. *m.* 'Album', whose flowers are blush-white rather than pure white; G. *m.* 'Ingwersen's Variety', with soft, mauve-pink flowers; and G. *m.* 'Bevan's Variety', with taller stems of vivid magenta-pink flowers.
Flowers Apr–Jul. Approx. height and spread 40 × 40 cm (16 × 16 in).

Stinking hellebore (*Helleborus foetidus*) sounds like a particularly unpleasant insult, but in fact it's a stunning plant for dry shade. It

Snowy mespilus
(*Amelanchier lamarckii*)
in spring.

makes neat clumps of deep green, sharply divided, fan-shaped leaves and bears clusters of small, pale green, bell-shaped flowers in winter.
Flowers Jan–Apr. Approx. height and spread 60 × 40 cm (2 ft × 16 in).

Dead nettle (*Lamium maculatum*) is useful ground cover in dry shade, which is probably the one place in the garden where you could plant its invasive relative, *Lamiastrum galeobdolon*, which has larger, variegated leaves. Dry shade prevents it from being too vigorous and swamping everything else in sight. (See page 71.)
Flowers May–Jun. Approx. height and spread 30 cm × 1 m + (1 × 3 ft +).

Lily-turf (*Liriope muscari*) has narrow, strap-like, evergreen leaves and, in autumn, spikes of violet-blue flowers that look like those of the grape hyacinth.
Flowers Aug–Oct. Approx. height and spread 40 × 40 cm (16 × 16 in).

Bowles' golden grass (*Milium effusum* 'Aureum') provides a real pool of sunshine in a shady spot, with its very fine golden leaves and sprays of tiny, gold, bead-like flowers in early summer. Beth Chatto grows it to great effect with the purple-leaved *Viola labradorica* and snowdrops.
Flowers Apr–May. Approx. height and spread 40 × 30 cm (16 × 12 in).

Lungwort (*Pulmonaria* species) does well in dry shade. (See page 73.)

Piggy-back plant (*Tolmeia menziesii* 'Variegata') is so called because it produces small plantlets on top of its leaves, which will root if carefully removed and pressed into the ground. It has very attractive, round, yellow-speckled leaves, and though it's often sold as a houseplant it's perfectly hardy. The flowers are insignificant.
Approx. height and spread 30 × 30 cm (1 × 1 ft).

Viola labradorica does well in dry shade, though it's not as invasive as it is in moister soil – no bad thing! (See page 74.)

Waldsteinia ternata is a lovely evergreen carpeter with glossy, dark green, three-lobed leaves, which sometimes take on a bronze tint in winter, and sprays of golden-yellow flowers, rather like strawberry flowers, in spring.
Flowers Apr–May. Approx. height and spread 8–10 cm × 1 m (3–5 in × 3 ft).

ANNUALS
No annuals will really thrive in dry shade, though if you have a few busy Lizzies (*Impatiens*) to spare it would be worth planting them out and taking a chance.

BULBS
Arum italicum 'Pictum' will grow well enough in dry shade beneath a wall provided there is some moisture below the surface and the bulbs are planted quite deep. (See page 75.)

Glory of the snow (*Chionodoxa luciliae*) will grow under deciduous trees or hedges. (See page 75.)

Meadow saffron (*Colchicum speciosum*) has pink, mauve or white flowers in September, and its leaves don't appear till spring. The flowers look rather strange sprouting from naked earth, so you could try planting them among ground-cover plants.
Flowers Sept. Approx. height 15–18 cm (6–7 in). Plant 10 cm (4 in) apart.

Cyclamen hederifolium is worth trying if you work plenty of organic matter into the top few inches of soil before planting. (See page 76.)

Snowdrops (*Galanthus nivalis*) are worth trying since they appear when there is most likely to be some moisture about. (See page 77.)

Bluebells (*Hyacinthoides non-scripta*) are also pretty tough and worth trying. They produce the classic blue flowers in spring and, if they are happy, will self-seed freely.
Flowers Apr–May. Approx. height 20 cm (8 in). Plant 8 cm (3 in) apart.

Ornithogalum nutans, a cousin of the star of Bethlehem, has very attractive, pale grey-green and white star-shaped flowers with petals that curve back.
Flowers Apr–May. Approx. height 15–40 cm (6–16 in). Plant 15 cm (6 in) apart.

Dense Shade

Those plants marked 'C' will also tolerate really heavy clay.

CLIMBERS
Ivy (*Hedera helix* and *H. colchicum*). C. (See page 58.)

SHRUBS
Spotted laurel (*Aucuba japonica* and *A. j.* 'Variegata'). C. (See page 59.)

False castor-oil plant (*Fatsia japonica*). (See page 60.)

Wintergreen (*Gaultheria procumbens*). (See page 54.)

Japanese privet (*Ligustrum japonicum*) has very glossy, dark green leaves and is not as attractive as other privets, but it will grow where they won't!
Average height and spread after five years 60×40 cm (2 ft × 16 in); after ten years 1.8×1 m ($5\frac{1}{2} \times 3$ ft).

Pachysandra terminalis and *P. t.* 'Variegata'. (See page 62.)

Cherry laurel (*Prunus laurocerasus* 'Otto Luyken'). C. (See page 82.)

Christmas box (*Sarcococca humilis*). (See page 63.)

Snowberry (*Symphoricarpos × doorenbosii*). C. (See page 66.)

Greater and lesser periwinkle (*Vinca major* and *V. minor*). C. (See page 82.)

HERBACEOUS PLANTS
Brunnera macrophylla. (See page 83.)

Lily-of-the-valley (*Convallaria majalis*), with its superbly scented flowers, can become almost a weed when it's established, though dense shade is likely to keep it under reasonable control.
Flowers Apr–May. Approx. height and spread 20×50 cm + (8 × 18 in +).

Spurge (*Euphorbia robbiae*). (See page 84.)

Above: Foxgloves
(*Digitalis*) thrive in shade
and tolerate most soil
types.

Right: The stinking
hellebore (*Helleborus
foetidus*) will tolerate dry
shade.

Spurge (*Euphorbia robbiae*) is another good plant for difficult, dry, shady sites.

Plantain lily – the variety *Hosta fortunei* only, with large, deeply ribbed, plain green leaves and mauve flowers, will thrive in dense shade provided the soil is always moist.
Flowers Jun–Aug. Approx. height and spread $75 \times 60\,cm$ ($2\frac{1}{2} \times 2\,ft$) C.

Dead nettle (*Lamium maculatum*/*Lamiastrum galeobdolon*). C. (See pages 71 and 85.)

Planting Plan for Dry Shade
(See illus. on pages 80–1.)

CLIMBERS
Allow 3 m (10 ft) for each plant.

1 *Hydrangea petiolaris*. Fresh spring leaf colour/early summer flowers. (See page 58.)

2 Ivy (*Hedera helix* 'Gold Heart'). Evergreen/bright variegation for winter colour. (See page 58.)

3 Virginia creeper (*Parthenocissus henryana*). Lovely foliage all summer/brilliant autumn colour. (See page 59.)

SHRUBS
A Spotted laurel (*Aucuba japonica* 'Variegata'). Evergreen/bright variegation for winter colour. (See page 59.)

B Guelder rose (*Viburnum opulus*, e.g. 'Notcutt's Variety'). Lovely white lace-cap flowers/translucent red berries in autumn. (See page 66.)

C Flowering currant (*Ribes sanguineum*). Fast-growing with attractive rose-red flowers in early summer. If the snowy mespilus and guelder rose outgrow their space after five years or so, the currant can be removed. (See page 82.)

D Snowy mespilus (*Amelanchier lamarckii*). Clouds of white flowers in spring and lovely autumn colour. This and the currant are both deciduous, so the variegated ivy behind takes over in winter months. (See page 78.)

E *Mahonia japonica*. Evergreen, with bright yellow flowers in winter before the Virginia creeper is in leaf. Its red tints in autumn tone with the Virginia creeper's. (See page 82.)

F Golden elder (*Sambucus nigra* 'Aurea'). A splash of gold in the corner. (See page 63.)

PERENNIALS AND SMALL SHRUBS

a 3 × stinking hellebore (*Helleborus foetidus*). The dark evergreen foliage will show up beautifully against the golden variegated laurel. (See page 84.)

b 3 × *Geranium macrorrhizum* 'Ingwersen's Variety'. Attractive pink flowers in early summer with aromatic, more or less evergreen foliage. (See page 84.)

c *Euonymus fortunei* 'Emerald and Gold'. A bright evergreen between two deciduous shrubs (guelder rose and flowering currant) will give winter colour, and the green and gold variegation will echo the ivy behind it to the right. (See page 79.)

d 3 × Japanese anemone (*Anemone × hybrida* 'Alba' or 'Honorine Jobert'). The white flowers will show up beautifully against the autumn colour of the snowy mespilus. (See page 67.)

e *Viburnum davidii*. This will form quite a large clump in ten years, but can be cut back. (See page 66.)

f 3 × foxglove (*Digitalis grandiflorum*). The bronze-tinged yellow flowers in summer will show up against the dark green of the mahonia. (See page 83.)

g 3 × spurge (*Euphorbia robbiae*). The dark green leaves will stand out well against the golden elder and the green-yellow flowers will tone with it. (See page 84.)

GROUND COVER AND BULBS

h 3 × elephant's ears (*Bergenia* 'Ballawley'). The large, round leaves form an ideal 'stop' to the border. (See page 70.)

i Lungwort (*Pulmonaria saccharata* 'Sissinghurst') has variegated leaves and pure white flowers. (See page 73.)

j 3 × eastern bleeding heart (*Dicentra eximia*). Its delicate, ferny foliage will contrast well with the elephant's ears and its flowers will take over once the latter's have finished. (See page 83.)

k 3 × Bowles' golden grass (*Milium effusum* 'Aureum'). A splash of brightness. (See page 85.)

l 3 × *Viola labradorica*. The purplish foliage contrasts beautifully with its golden neighbour (and with its other ferny, light green neighbour!). Plant snowdrops between Cc and Dd, and between the individual plants in each group. (See page 74.)

m 3 × *Hosta* 'Thomas Hogg'. Lovely cream-edged leaves. (See page 71.)

n 3 × *Lamium maculatum* 'White Nancy'. The silvery variegated foliage will look marvellous next to the *Viola labradorica* and in front of the dark green spurge. (See page 71.)

o *Hosta sieboldiana* 'Elegans'. Its huge, rounded, ribbed, blue-green leaves are an excellent contrast with its neighbours. (See page 71.)

p Lily-turf (*Liriope muscari*). (See page 85.)

q 3 × lady's mantle (*Alchemilla mollis*). Another good 'stop' plant; though its leaves aren't as big as the elephant's ears, they're much bigger than the dead nettle's or the viola's. The yellow-green flowers will tone with the spurge and the foliage of the golden elder. (See page 67.)

r Busy Lizzie (*Impatiens*) in its pale pink form is well worth trying here. (See page 74.)

Plant *Cyclamen hederifolium* between m and n – its flowers will show up well against the silvery dead nettle foliage, and the dark green leaves, marbled silver, which follow will contrast with it – and between i and j. Plant snowdrops between k and l.

CHAPTER FIVE

East-facing borders

In a border that faces east, and gets sun for the first part of the day, you can grow many plants that are happy in partial shade, as you can in a west-facing border. The main difference between the two is that a border facing east is cooler – for one thing, the early morning sun doesn't have as much heat in it as the afternoon sun; and for another, winds from the east can be bitingly cold. That rules out plants that are slightly tender like trumpet vine (*Campsis radicans*) and many hebes.

East-facing borders are also not ideal for plants like camellias (even if you have an acid soil) or winter-flowering jasmine. In cold weather the buds freeze, and if they are allowed to thaw out slowly as they would on a north-facing wall, they survive undamaged, but if they are exposed to early-morning sun, as they would be in an east-facing border, and thaw too fast, they are damaged, turn brown and fall off.

However, as always in gardening, there are compensations. Many of the superb, large, pale pink, mauve or striped clematises, like the very popular, pale pink-mauve and carmine, 'Nelly Moser', the lavender-mauve 'Barbara Jackman', or the raspberry-pink 'Carnaby', keep their colour much better on an east-facing wall than they do in full sun, which tends to bleach it out.

Another group of plants that do very well in east-facing borders are those with golden foliage. As Rosemary Verey says, it's quite hard to strike a balance between too much sun, which can scorch some golden foliage quite badly, and too little, in which case the brilliant gold colour fades to a golden-green. But an east-facing border, which gets full sun in the morning, and loses it at around the middle of the day before it's too fierce for too long, is ideal.

Golden foliage is very attractive in that setting, too, lit up by the early-morning sun. East light can be a little cold so a shrub like the golden-leafed mock orange (*Philadelphus coronarius* 'Aurea') or the small, box-leafed honeysuckle (*Lonicera nitida* 'Baggesen's Gold'), which creates its own warmth and brightness, is ideal.

Ivy (*Hedera helix* 'Goldheart').

If you do decide to make your east-facing border a golden one, you can't simply plant nothing but shrubs and herbaceous plants with gold foliage, as a garden at a recent Chelsea Flower Show demonstrated quite clearly. In order to show off golden foliage to its best advantage you need a fair proportion of plain greens – light as well as dark – and a few variegated plants too. Otherwise you'll wind up with whatever the golden equivalent is of the type of all-grey foliage garden Beth Chatto describes as 'an ash heap'! When it comes to flower colour, you can choose what you like, but as Rosemary Verey's gold border shows, white, and yellow, with just a touch of blue looks very effective indeed. As well as many excellent deciduous trees and shrubs with golden foliage, there are some evergreens – or perhaps 'evergolds' would be a more accurate description – as well. Apart from *Lonicera nitida* 'Baggesen's Gold', there's the new golden form of Mexican orange blossom (*Choisya ternata* 'Sundance') and the low-growing Japanese holly (*Ilex crenata* 'Golden Gem') – ideal for this situation since it needs sun to achieve its brightest colour, but is very prone to damage from scorching.

The majority of golden evergreens, however, are conifers, though that's not to say the reverse is true, for there are excellent conifers for small gardens in every shade of green and blue as well. They come in a wide range of shapes and sizes – bun shapes, mop-heads, pillars, pyramids, cones – and you want to be doubly sure that the little specimen you're buying is in fact a dwarf or very slow-growing conifer and not simply a very young giant! Some change colour as the seasons pass – *Thuja occidentalis* 'Rheingold', for example, turns from gold to coppery-gold in the winter, while the smaller *T. orientalis* 'Golden Ball' is bright yellow in spring and summer, turning green and sometimes bronze in autumn and winter. Most conifers prefer a slightly acid or neutral soil, though junipers and yew will tolerate lime.

As already explained, though, an east border, especially in an exposed garden, can be very cold, and some conifers, particularly when first planted, can be badly scorched by biting winds. They lose so much moisture as a result of the wind drying out their foliage that in effect they are suffering from drought and so the leaves turn brown. It's vital, therefore, that you give them some winter protection, either by planting them in the lee of other, larger, tougher shrubs which will act as a windbreak or by making a temporary windbreak from perforated plastic material made specially for the purpose. Don't try to make a solid windbreak: for one thing, it's liable to blow down; and for another, what happens is that the wind hits it, whips over the top and swirls and eddies on the other side, doing just the kind of damage to the plants that you set out to prevent.

In this chapter the plants with golden foliage are listed in each section (the first deals with plants for reasonably moisture-retentive soils, the second with those for dry soils) as well as some particularly suitable contrast plants.

Moist Soil

TREES

Golden birch (*Betula* 'Golden Cloud') is a golden 'silver' birch which develops the lovely white bark associated with the species within a few years. It can be grown as a small tree or as a shrub if you prune it back in winter. Left alone, it is expected to reach 5 × 4 m (16 × 13 ft) in twenty years.

Golden honey locust (*Gleditsia triacanthos* 'Sunburst'). (See page 50.)

Golden Indian bean tree (*Catalpa bignonioides* 'Aurea'). (See page 50.)

Golden false acacia (*Robinia pseudacacia* 'Frisia'). Its branches are brittle and vulnerable to wind damage, so it needs a sheltered position. (See page 48.)

CLIMBERS
Golden foliage
Japanese honeysuckle (*Lonicera japonica* 'Aureo-reticulata') in fact has variegated gold and green leaves, but from a distance they look gold. It also has yellow flowers. (See page 58.)

Golden ivy (*Hedera helix* 'Buttercup') has small, bright golden-yellow leaves, while *H.h.* 'Goldheart' has large, central gold splashes on its leaves, as does the much larger-leafed Persian ivy (*H. colchica* 'Paddy's Pride'). (See page 58.)

Golden hop (*Humulus lupulus* 'Aureus') is a vigorous climber, grown primarily for its foliage which colours best in full sun. Prune it back hard each spring to ensure the brightest foliage colour and to keep it in bounds.
Approx. height (in one season) 4–5 m (13–16 ft).

Contrasts
Irish ivy (*Hedera helix* 'Hibernica'), with its large, dark green leaves, also makes a superb backdrop for a golden-leafed shrub.

Climbing hydrangea (*Hydrangea petiolaris*) – again! – with its bright green foliage and flat heads of white flowers. (See page 58.)

American honeysuckle (*Lonicera americana*) has white and yellow flowers all summer. (See page 58.) The Chinese woodbine (*L. tragophylla*) has dark green leaves and bright golden-yellow flowers in June and July. It will cope with dense shade, and grows up to 6 m (20 ft).

SHRUBS WITH GOLDEN FOLIAGE
Barberry (*Berberis thunbergii* 'Aurea'), which forms a medium-sized spreading shrub, has bright gold foliage in spring fading to pale green by the end of the summer and then turning orange-gold in autumn. It needs protection both from frosts and icy winds and from hot sun. (See page 78.)

Mexican orange blossom (*Choisya ternata* 'Sundance') is a new golden-leafed form. Unlike its parent it won't do well in full shade, but like its parent needs shelter from cold winds. It has the same white flowers, though some people find them not as strongly scented. (See page 140.)

Dogwood (*Cornus alba*) has a golden form, *C.a.* 'Aurea', with soft butter-coloured leaves. Alternatively, you could choose the gold-and-green-variegated 'Spaethii', which looks gold from a distance, and which has brighter red stems in winter. (See page 60.)

45. *Cimicifuga simplex*

59. *Hedera helix hibernica*

8. Clematis 'Comtesse de Bouchard'

44. *Campanula lactiflora*

22. *Rosa rubrifolia*

42. Ajuga 'Burgundy Glow'

21. *Viburnum davidii*

23. Fuchsia 'Tom Thumb'

43. *Bergenia* 'Ballawley'

39. *Choysia ternata*
'Sundance'

13. *Sorbus cashmiriana*

9. *Actinidia*
kolomikta

25. *Philadelphus*
coronarius
'Aureus'

40. *Dianthus*
deltoides

38. *Allium*
schoenoprasum
'Forescate'

41. *Saponaria*
ocymoides

24. *Skimmia japonica*
'Rubella'

Winter-flowering heathers (*Erica carnea*), which are tolerant of lime, include a number of varieties with bright gold foliage in winter. Look for *E.c.* 'Aurea', 'Foxhollow', 'January Sun' and 'Westwood Yellow'.

Golden fuchsia (*Fuchsia magallanica* 'Aurea') has the brightest golden foliage in full sun, but in partial shade it's still very attractive. It has small red flowers in midsummer. If the frost doesn't cut it back, prune it hard in spring for brighter foliage.
Flowers Jun–Aug. Approx. height and spread in one season 1×1 m (3×3 ft).

Japanese holly (*Ilex crenata* 'Golden Gem') is a low, spreading, evergreen shrub with small golden leaves which turn green in their second year, though the new growth is always golden. (A standard-sized variegated holly, like 'Golden King', which is as much gold as green, would qualify here too – see page 79.)
Approx. height and spread after five years 40×80 cm (16 ins $\times 2\frac{1}{2}$ ft); after ten years 60 cm $\times 1$ m (2×3 ft).

Box-leafed honeysuckle (*Lonicera nitida* 'Baggesen's Gold') makes a small, 'evergold', rather untidy shrub which works well in mixed, informal planting. It seems to become brighter gold in winter.
Approx. height and spread after five years 60 cm $\times 1.2$ m (2×4 ft); after ten years 1.2×2 m (4×6 ft).

Mock orange (*Philadelphus coronarius* 'Aureus') has bright yellow foliage in spring turning to yellow-green as the summer progresses. It has fragrant, white flowers in midsummer. (See page 146.)

Flowering currant (*Ribes sanguineum*) has a golden form, 'Brocklebankii', which has pale pink flowers. (See page 82.)

Golden elder (*Sambucus nigra* 'Aurea') and cut-leafed golden elder (*Sambucus racemosa* 'Plumosa Aurea', or the even hardier new form *S.r.* 'Sutherland') are excellent shrubs for this border. (See page 63.)

Spiraea has two excellent golden forms: *S. bumalda* 'Gold Flame' and the newer *S. japonica* 'Golden Princess'. (See page 148.)

Guelder rose (*Viburnum opulus*) has a golden form, *V.o.* 'Aureum'. (See page 66.)

GOLDEN CONIFERS
Chamaecyparis lawsoniana 'Mimima Aurea' makes a rounded pyramid of golden foliage all year.
Approx. height and spread (at the base) after ten years 60×50 cm ($2 \times 1\frac{1}{2}$ ft).

Ch. obtusa 'Nana Lutea' is a slow-growing, spreading bush that keeps its golden colour all year.
Approx. height and spread after ten years 50 × 30 cm ($1\frac{1}{2}$ × 1 ft).

Ch. pisifera 'Sungold' makes a golden-yellow mop-head as broad as it's high.
Approx. height and spread after ten years 60 × 60 cm (2 × 2 ft).

Junipers are among the hardiest conifers and will tolerate chalky soil. Some of the golden forms, like *Juniperus communis* 'Depressa Aurea', need full sun to give of their best, but others are happy in partial shade. *J.* × *media* 'Gold Coast', which retains its colour through the winter, makes a spreading bush, wider than it is high.
Approx. height and spread after ten years 75 cm × 1.2 m ($2\frac{1}{2}$ × 4 ft).

J. × *media* **'Gold Sovereign'**, a new introduction, is the smallest of the semi-prostrate golden junipers.
Approx. height and spread after ten years 50–75 cm (18 in × $2\frac{1}{2}$ ft).

Mountain pine (*Pinus mugo*) is a superb small conifer with long, fine pine 'needles'. *P.m.* 'Wintergold' is a deep golden-yellow throughout the winter, turning a light green in summer.
Approx. height and spread after ten years 40 × 90 cm (16 in × 3 ft).

Yew (*Taxus baccata*) offers two excellent golden forms: the lovely, old gold, narrow, upright *T.b.* 'Standishii', 1 m × 30 cm (3 × 1 ft), and the low, spreading 'Summergold' (which as its name suggests has its brightest gold colouring in summer), 50 cm × 1.4 m (18 in × $4\frac{1}{2}$ ft).

Thujas are tolerant of most soil types, including a degree of lime, as long as they are not too wet.

Thuja occidentalis 'Rheingold' has a rounded, conical shape and foliage that is gold in summer and coppery-gold in winter.
Approx. height and spread after ten years 1 m × 80 cm (3 × $2\frac{1}{2}$ ft).

T. occidentalis 'Sunkist' eventually makes a pyramid of foliage that stays bright gold all year round.
Approx. height and spread after ten years 1.2 m × 60 cm (4 × 2 ft).

T. orientalis 'Aurea Nana' makes a superb, small, oval bush, golden-yellow in early summer and yellow or even bronze-green in winter.
Approx. height and spread after ten years 60 × 30 cm (2 × 1 ft).

T. orientalis 'Collen's Gold' is a pillar of golden foliage all year.
Approx. height and spread after ten years 1.2 m × 50 cm (4 × $1\frac{1}{2}$ ft).

Winter-flowering heather (*Erica carnea* 'Westwood Yellow').

T. orientalis **'Golden Ball'** makes a dome-shaped bush, bright gold in late spring and summer, green and sometimes bronze in autumn and winter.

Approx. height and spread after ten years 40 × 40 cm (16 × 16 in).

T. orientalis **'Pyramidalis Aurea',** as its name suggests, makes a narrow pyramid of golden-yellow foliage.

Approx. height after ten years 2 m (6 ft).

SHRUBS FOR CONTRAST

Spotted laurel (*Aucuba japonica*) in its plain form or one of the less brightly variegated forms like *A.j.* 'Variegata'. (See page 59.)

Dogwood (*Cornus*) in non-golden forms. (See page 60.)

Cotoneaster, in its ground-hugging forms, like *Cotoneaster dammeri* which has deep green, evergreen foliage, provides good contrast to golden foliage. (See page 141.)

Elaeagnus × *ebbingei* and *E. pungens* 'Maculata'. (See page 115.)

Spindle (*Euonymus fortunei*), especially the gold-and-green-variegated forms like 'Emerald and Gold' and the dwarf 'Sunspot'. (See page 79.)

Chinese witch hazel (*Hamamelis mollis*) has sweetly scented, yellow flowers in winter – attractive with 'evergold' foliage. (See page 61.)

Mahonia japonica. (See page 82.)

Osmanthus burkwoodii (formerly *Osmarea burkwoodii*) is similar to *Osmanthus delavayi* only larger and tougher.
Flowers Apr–May. Approx. height and spread 2–3 m × 2–3 m (6–10 ft × 6–10 ft).

Photinia × *fraseri* **'Red Robin'.**
Approx. height and spread after 5 years 1.5 × 2 m (5 × 6 ft).

Potentilla fruticosa. (See page 146.)

Cherry laurel (*Prunus laurocerasus* 'Otto Luyken'), with its glossy, dark, evergreen leaves, is an excellent contrast to golden foliage. It can be pruned to keep it small. (See page 82.)

Firethorn (*Pyracantha* species) is a good, evergreen wall shrub for east-facing borders. (See page 62.)

Christmas box (*Sarcococca humilis*). (See page 63.)

Skimmia is another valuable evergreen, and, if plants of both sexes are grown, red berries in winter result. (See page 63.)

Above: Golden creeping Jenny (*Lysimachia nummularia* 'Aurea').

Cut-leafed golden elder (*Sambucus racemosa* 'Plumosa Aurea').

Viburnums include some very hardy specimens: the winter-flowering *Viburnum tinus*; the spring-flowering *V. × burkwoodii* and *V. plicatum tomentosum* 'Mariesii'; and the evergreens, grown largely for their foliage, *V. rhytidophyllum* (if you have plenty of room) and the much smaller *V. davidii*. (See page 66.)

HERBACEOUS PLANTS
Golden foliage

Golden feverfew (*Chrysanthemum parthenium* 'Aureum') forms small mounds of finely cut, yellow leaves covered with small white daisies throughout the summer. It does best in full sun but grows well enough in an east-facing border, provided the soil isn't too wet or heavy.
Flowering Jun–Sept. Approx. height and spread 30 × 20 cm (1 ft × 8 in).

Hosta fortunei 'Aurea' has lovely, soft, butter-yellow leaves in spring, slowly fading through the summer to light green. *H.f.* 'Albopicta' is a variegated form whose leaves are marbled with yellow, gold and just a little green. Both must have partial shade, and both have lilac flowers from midsummer onwards. (See page 71.)

Dead nettle (*Lamium maculatum* 'Aureum') is a very valuable ground-cover plant for moist soils, and will tolerate quite dense shade. (See page 71.)

Creeping Jenny (*Lysimachia nummularia* 'Aurea') is another good ground-cover plant for damp soil, with long trailing stems of round, golden leaves and yellow flowers in summer.
Flowers Jun–Jul. Approx. height and spread 5 × 60 cm (2 in × 2 ft).

Lemon balm (*Melissa officinalis* 'Aurea') has rich yellow leaves. (See page 119.)

Bowles' golden grass (*Milium effusum* 'Aureum') has foliage, stems and flowers which are all golden yellow. (See page 85.)

Contrasts

Monkshood (*Aconitum* species). (See page 66.)

Lady's mantle (*Alchemilla mollis*). (See page 67.)

Japanese anemone (*Anemone × hybrida*). (See page 67.)

Columbine (*Aquilegia* species). (See page 67.)

Astilbe. (See page 67.)

Masterwort (*Astrantia major*). (See page 67.)

Elephant's ears (*Bergenia* species). (See page 70.)

Bugbane (*Cimicifuga* species). (See page 70.)

Hellebores (*Helleborus niger* and *H. orientalis*). (See pages 70–1.)

Day lilies (*Hemerocallis* species). (See page 155.)

Hostas. (See page 71.)

Houttuynia cordata. (See page 155.)

Knotweed (*Polygonum affine* and *P. bistorta*). (See page 72.)

Primulas. (See page 73.)

Lungwort (*Pulmonaria* species). (See page 73.)

Rodgersias (*R. pinnata* and *R. podophylla*) are superb, large, bold, foliage plants for a semi-shaded, moist border. Plumes of small pink or cream flowers rise above the mound of foliage. They need a spot sheltered from strong winds.
Flowers Jul. Approx. height and spread 1 m × 80 cm ($3 \times 2\frac{1}{2}$ ft).

ANNUALS
Almost all the traditional annuals will do well in this situation, except the few like Livingstone daisy (*Mesembryanthemum*) which really like it hot and dry. Since there are none which have foliage that is truly golden, you can simply choose on the basis of flower colours that fit your scheme.

BULBS
All the usual spring-flowering bulbs will do well here too, though it won't be hot enough for exotics like the belladonna lily (*Amaryllis belladonna*). Again, there are no bulbs with golden foliage, so let flower colour dictate your choice.

Dry Soil

Again the list is much shorter than that for moist soil, but even so there are enough golden-leafed plants to give you the effect you want.

TREES
Silver birch (*Betula* 'Golden Cloud'). (See page 48.)

Right: Japanese honeysuckle (*Lonicera japonica* 'Aureo-reticulata').

Far right: Mountain pine (*Pinus mugo* 'Wintergold').

Below: Prunus laurocerasus 'Otto Luyken'.

Left: Golden balm
(*Melissa officinalis*
'Aurea').

Below: The nasturtium
(*Tropaeolum majus*) is
one of the few annuals
that thrives in poor, dry
soil and part-shade.

Honey locust (*Gleditsia triacanthos* 'Sunburst'). (See page 50.)

CLIMBERS
Ivy (*Hedera helix* and *H. colchica*). (See page 58.)

Japanese honeysuckle (*Lonicera japonica* 'Aureo-reticulata') prefers a moister soil, but if you add organic matter when you plant, and mulch it well afterwards, it should do well enough. (See page 58.)

SHRUBS
Golden privet (*Ligustrum ovalifolium* 'Aureum') is evergreen and will grow well in conditions where many others won't.
Flowers Jul. Approx. height and spread 4–5 m × 4–5 m (12–15 ft × 12–15 ft).

Box-leafed honeysuckle (*Lonicera nitida* 'Baggesen's Gold'). (See page 98.)

Mock orange (*Philadelphus coronarius* 'Aureus') will tolerate dry soil if you add plenty of organic matter when you plant it and mulch it well afterwards. (See page 146.)

Flowering currant (*Ribes sanguineum* 'Brocklebankii'). (See page 82.)

Golden elder (*Sambucus nigra* 'Aurea') and golden cut-leafed elder (*S. racemosa* 'Plumosa Aurea'). (See page 63.)

CONIFERS
The golden varieties of **Chamaecyparis lawsoniana** listed on page 98 (provided you add plenty of organic matter when you plant), of *Juniper × media*, *Taxus baccata* and *Thuja occidentalis* and *T. orientalis* should all do well.

Contrasts
Barberry (*Berberis* species), in some of its evergreen forms, will cope well enough. (See page 78.)

Spindle (*Euonymus fortunei*), especially the gold-and-green-variegated forms, will do well, but you must be prepared to mulch and even water in the first season. (See page 79.)

Holly (*Ilex × altaclarensis*). *I. aquifolium* in one of its plain green forms, like 'J.C. van Tol', or golden and green variegated forms, like 'Golden King', is also a valuable evergreen. (See page 79.)

Mahonia japonica or *M. aquifolium*. (See page 82.)

Skimmia. (See page 63.)

HERBACEOUS PLANTS

Golden foliage

Spurge (*Euphorbia robbiae*) has large heads of yellow-green flowers and, from a distance, the effect is yellow. (See page 84.) *E. polychroma* has green foliage but such large heads of sulphur-yellow flowers in spring that the overall effect is also of a golden plant. Flowers Apr–May. Approx. height and spread 40 × 30 cm (16 in × 1 ft).

Dead nettle (*Lamium maculatum* 'Aureum'). (See page 71.)

Lemon balm (*Melissa officinalis* 'Aurea'). (See page 119.)

Bowles' golden grass (*Milium effusum* 'Aureum'), provided you add plenty of organic matter when planting. (See page 85.)

Piggy-back plant (*Tolmeia menziesii* 'Variegata') looks more yellow than green. (See page 86.)

Contrasts

Lady's mantle (*Alchemilla mollis*). (See page 67.)

Elephant's ears (*Bergenia* species). (See page 70.)

Foxglove (*Digitalis* species). (See page 83.)

Barrenwort (*Epimedium* species). (See page 84.)

Cranesbill, especially *Geranium macrorrhizum*. (See page 84.)

Stinking hellebore (*Helleborus foetidus*). (See page 84.)

Lily-turf (*Liriope muscari*). (See page 85.)

Viola labradorica. (See page 86.)

Waldsteinia ternata. (See page 86.)

ANNUALS

Thank god for nasturtiums! Most of the other annuals that will thrive in poor, dry soils like gazanias and Livingstone daisies (*Mesembryanthemum*) are sun lovers that open their flowers only in full sun.

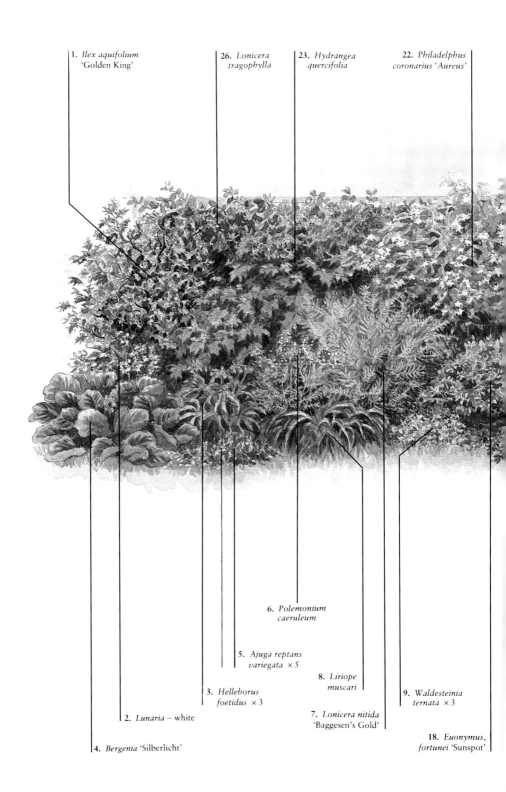

1. *Ilex aquifolium* 'Golden King'

26. *Lonicera tragophylla*

23. *Hydrangea quercifolia*

22. *Philadelphus coronarius* 'Aureus'

6. *Polemonium caeruleum*

5. *Ajuga reptans variegata* × 5

8. *Liriope muscari*

3. *Helleborus foetidus* × 3

9. *Waldesteinia ternata* × 3

2. *Lunaria* – white

7. *Lonicera nitida* 'Baggesen's Gold'

18. *Euonymus, fortunei* 'Sunspot'

4. *Bergenia* 'Silberlicht'

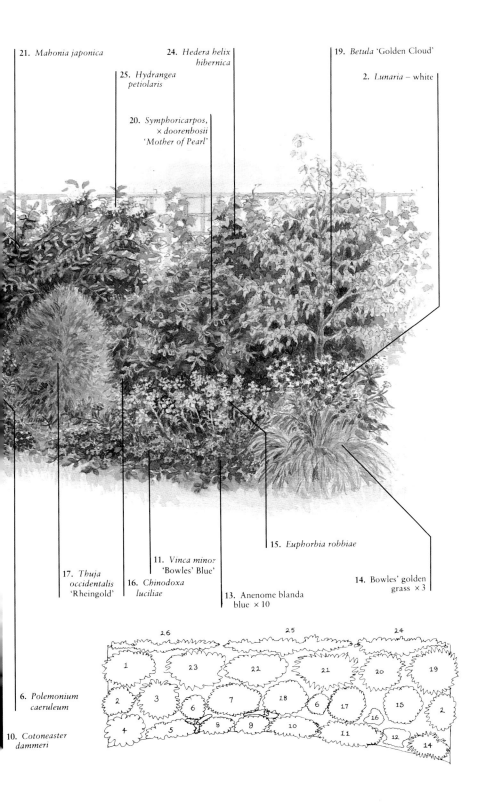

21. *Mahonia japonica*

24. *Hedera helix hibernica*

19. *Betula* 'Golden Cloud'

25. *Hydrangea petiolaris*

2. *Lunaria* – white

20. *Symphoricarpos, × doorenbosii* 'Mother of Pearl'

15. *Euphorbia robbiae*

17. *Thuja occidentalis* 'Rheingold'

11. *Vinca minor* 'Bowles' Blue'

16. *Chinodoxa luciliae*

13. Anenome blanda blue × 10

14. Bowles' golden grass × 3

6. *Polemonium caeruleum*

10. *Cotoneaster dammeri*

BULBS

Few bulbs really like these conditions, but if you add organic matter to the soil before planting, the following are well worth trying.

Anemone blanda. (See page 163.)

Autumn crocus (*Crocus autumnale*).
Flowers Sept–Oct. Approx. height 5– 12 cm (2–5 in). Plant 8 cm (3 in) apart.

Crocus. (See page 164.)

Glory of the snow (*Chionodoxa luciliae*). (See page 75.)

Grape hyacinth (*Muscari* species). (See page 77.)

Ornithogalum nutans. (See page 87.)

Planting Plan for a Dry, East-facing Border
(See Illus. on pages 108–9.)

CLIMBERS
Allow 3 m (10 ft) for each plant.

1 Chinese woodbine (*Lonicera tragophylla*). Glowing gold flowers in June–July, followed by red berries for autumn colour. (See page 95.)

2 *Hydrangea petiolaris*. (See page 58.)

3 Irish ivy (*Hedera helix* 'Hibernica'). Glossy, evergreen leaves. (See page 95.)

SHRUBS
A Holly (*Ilex aquifolium* 'Golden King'). (See page 79.)

B Oak-leafed hydrangea (*Hydrangea quercifolia*). White flowers and good autumn colour. (See page 62.)

C Mock orange (*Philadelphus coronarius* 'Aureus'). (See page 146.)

D *Mahonia japonica.* (See page 82.)

E Snowberry (*Symphoricarpus × doorenbosii* 'Mother of Pearl'). Pink berries in autumn show up well against the ivy. (See page 66.)

F Golden birch (*Betula* 'Golden Cloud') grown as a shrub about 2 m (6 ft) high. (See page 94.)

PERENNIALS AND SMALL SHRUBS

a 3 × Stinking hellebore (*Helleborus foetidus*). (See page 84.)

b Box-leafed honeysuckle (*Lonicera nitida* 'Baggesen's Gold'). Bright against the hydrangea. (See page 98.)

c Spindle (*Euonymus fortunei* 'Sunspot'). (See page 79.)

d *Thuja occidentalis* 'Rheingold'. A lovely contrast with the evergreen ivy in winter. (See page 99.)

e 3 × spurge (*Euphorbia robbiae*). Dark green leaves and yellow-green bracts tone well. (See page 84.)

f 3 × elephant's ears (*Bergenia* 'Silberlicht'). Pure white flowers in spring, turning faintly pink with age. (See page 70.)

g 5 × bugle (*Ajuga reptans* 'Variegata'). Beige and green leaves and intense blue flowers in spring. (See page 83.)

h 3 × lily-turf (*Liriope muscari*). Grass-like foliage and spikes of mauve-blue flowers in late summer. (See page 85.)

i *Waldsteinia ternata*. Attractive, evergreen, mat-forming foliage and buttercup-yellow flowers in spring. (See page 86.)

j *Cotoneaster dammeri*. Ground-hugging with white flowers in spring and red berries in autumn. (See page 141.)

k 3 × Lesser periwinkle (*Vinca minor* 'Bowles' Blue'). Evergreen trailer with small leaves and blue flowers in spring. (See page 82.)

l 3 × Bowles' golden grass (*Milium effusum* 'Aureum'). Add plenty of organic matter before planting. (See page 85.)

m Jacob's ladder (*Polemonium caeruleum*). (See page 156.)

n White variegated honesty (*Lunaria biennis variegata* 'Alba'). Flowers Apr–Jun. Approx. height and spread 60 × 30 cm (2 × 1 ft).

BULBS

Anemone blanda – white and blue. (See page 163.)

Glory of the snow (*Chionodoxa luciliae*). (See page 75.)

CHAPTER SIX

West-facing borders

When it comes to choosing the plants for a west-facing border – one which gets the sun from the middle of the day until late evening – bear in mind that many of those which will thrive in south-facing borders are suitable here too. The exceptions are the relatively few plants that need full sun. So when you are designing your west-facing border, other factors need to be considered.

Many people who are out at work all day (or, indeed involved in looking after small children at home) can really enjoy their garden only in the evening. Since the west-facing border is the one which gets the sun until latest in the evening, it makes sense to create some kind of sitting-out area near it, even if it's only a bench on the lawn, and concentrate on plants that give of their best then.

Certain colours look better in evening light than others – bright reds, acid yellows and deep purples are lost, whereas white, cream, pale yellow and the palest pinks seem to gleam in the half-light, as does silvery foliage. Then there are those plants whose flowers open in the evening, like the evening primrose (*Oenothera* species) and those whose fragrance is at its best at that time – climbers like honeysuckle, jasmine and the evergreen climbing species rose, *Rosa banksiae*, which smells of sweet violets; and perennials and annuals like sweet rocket (*Hesperis matronalis*), tobacco plants (*Nicotiana* species) and night-scented stocks (*Matthiola bicornis*). Interestingly, many of the plants most fragrant in the evening are white, pale pink, mauve or blue – colours that attract moths rather than butterflies, which prefer brighter colours on the whole, and of course moths come out only after the sun has gone down. Don't forget all the plants with aromatic foliage either – not only culinary herbs like rosemary, sage and thyme, but also others like artemisia, lavender, caryopteris and so on. If you spray them with the hose on a warm summer evening, the fragrance just wafts up in waves. For this reason we decided to make the west-facing border our fragrant border, and to stick largely to colours that look their best in the evening light.

Jasmine (*Jasminum officinale*).

   Again, when classifying the plants that you might use, the most useful division seems to be between borders with moisture-retentive but reasonably well-drained soil (clay soils where the drainage has been improved, sandy soils whose ability to retain moisture has been improved, as well as medium loam) and those with poor, dry soil. Once again, the plants that must have an acid soil are listed separately from those that will cope with really heavy clay.

Fragrant Plants Needing Acid Soil

Sweetspire (*Itea ilicifolia*). (See page 134.)

Pieris floribunda has very intensely fragrant flowers between March and May. (See page 55.)

Rhododendrons are mostly unscented but with a few notable exceptions. *Rhododendron luteum* has fragrant orange-yellow flowers in early summer, while a number of white-flowered hybrids like 'Angelo', 'Midsummer Snow' and 'Polar Bear' also have very sweetly scented flowers. Deciduous, Ghent hybrid azaleas, like the pink-flowered 'Norma', the soft yellow 'Narcissiflora' and the even paler 'Daviesii' have fragrant flowers too. (See page 55.)

Fragrant Plants for Moist Soil

TREES

Ornamental crabs (*Malus floribunda* and *M. hupehensis*) have sweetly scented flowers in spring. (See page 40.)

Flowering cherry (*Prunus* × *yedoensis*) has lovely almond-scented blossom in spring. (See page 43.)

CLIMBERS

Clematis montana has almond-scented white flowers, while *C.m.* 'Elizabeth' has soft pink, fragrant blooms. Both are very vigorous and should be let loose only where space allows. (See page 58.)

Jasmine (*Jasminum officinale*) will produce masses of pure white sweetly scented flowers from summer till autumn. *J.* × *stephanense* produces even more sweetly scented flowers, but for a shorter period. (See page 136.)

Honeysuckle (*Lonicera*) has many strongly scented varieties. Among the best are *Lonicera* × *americana*, with honey-scented flowers; *L. heckrottii*, with a similar scent but with yellow rather than cream flowers; and the early and late Dutch honeysuckles (*L. periclymenum* 'Belgica' and *L.p.* 'Serotina'), which between them produce fragrant flowers from May to September. Though they are fragrant in the day, the scent is more intense in the evening and at night. Moths love it. (See page 58.)

Roses are a must for a fragrant border. Many are scented, but among those that combine the very long flowering period that you want in a small garden with good fragrance are the pink 'Aloha', 'Pink Perpétue' and 'Zéphirine Drouhin', the yellow 'Maigold' and the apricot-pink 'Compassion'. Make an exception for the vigorous, violet-scented *Rosa banksiae* – the yellow-flowered 'Lutea', the double white 'Alba Plena' which flowers from April to June, or 'Albéric Barbier' with creamy white flowers. (See page 59.)

Wisteria floribunda and *W. sinensis* have vanilla-scented flowers. (See page 138.)

SHRUBS

Artemisias all have aromatic foliage. (See page 139.)

Buddleias (*Buddleia davidii*, *B. fallowiana* and *B.f.* 'Lochinch') have a musky, honey-like scent which butterflies love. (See page 139.)

Blue spiraea (*Caryopteris incana*) has aromatic foliage. (See page 167.)

Wintersweet (*Chimonanthus praecox*) has small, yellow, very sweetly scented flowers on bare stems in winter. Tolerates alkaline soil.
Flowers Feb–Mar. Approx. height and spread after 5 years 1.2 × 1 m (4 × 3 ft); after 10 years 2 × 1.5 m (6 × 5 ft).

Mexican orange blossom (*Choisya ternata*) not only has very fragrant flowers but its evergreen foliage gives off a pungent, rather peppery smell when you rub it between your fingers. (See page 140.)

Moroccan broom (*Cytisus battandieri*) has bright yellow flowers that smell like ripe pineapple. (See page 136.)

Broom (*Cytisis fragrans* or *C. × praecox*) also has fragrant flowers. (See page 142.)

Daphne has a number of forms which, between them, produce fragrant flowers from November to August. The best include *Daphne mezereum*, which has very fragrant, pale mauve-pink to purple-red flowers from January to March; *D. odora*, which has even more fragrant, pale pink flowers from February to April (the variegated form *D.o.* 'Aureo-marginata' which has the same sweetly scented pink flowers is better value in a small garden); and *D. cneorum*, which has very fragrant, tubular pink flowers in May and June. (See page 142.)

Elaeagnus, in all its varieties, is usually grown for its foliage. However, many forms, when they are mature, have small but sweetly scented flowers in summer/early autumn. Of the deciduous varieties look for *Elaeagnus angustifolia*, with long, silvery, willow-like leaves and very fragrant, yellow flowers in June, and *E. commutata*, with small, silver, slightly wavy leaves and very fragrant, silvery flowers in May. Among the evergreens, look for *E. × ebbingei*, with silver-green leaves, or the green-and-gold-variegated *E. pungens* 'Maculata', which is widely available; both of these flower eventually, in autumn.
Flowers May–Nov. Approx. height and spread after five years 1.2 × 1.2 m (4 × 4 ft); after ten years 2 × 2 m (6 × 6 ft).

Mount Etna broom (*Genista aetnensis*) is smothered in golden flowers smelling of vanilla in midsummer. (See page 169.)

Chinese witch hazel (*Hamamelis mollis*) carries very strongly scented, yellow, spider-like flowers on bare wood in winter. *H.m.* 'Pallida' has paler flowers and a less cloying scent. (See page 61.)

Lavender (*Lavandula* species) has scented flowers. (See page 170.)

Repeat-flowering,
scented climbing rose
'Maigold'.

Lemon verbena (*Lippia citriodora*) is worth growing simply for the pleasure of rubbing a leaf or two between your palms and sniffing! You can also use it for tea. It's not totally hardy, so plant it close to the wall or fence and shelter it from cold winds. If the frost doesn't cut it back for you, cut the stems to ground level in spring to encourage new aromatic foliage.
Flowers Aug. Approx. height and spread in one season 80×80 cm ($2\frac{1}{2} \times 2\frac{1}{2}$ ft).

Winter honeysuckle (*Lonicera fragrantissima*) has very fragrant, small, white flowers on almost bare branches during mild spells from autumn to early spring. Though rather spreading when young, it will eventually form a rounded shrub.
Flowers Nov–Mar. Approx. height and spread after five years 1.2×2 m (4×6 ft); after ten years 2×3 m (6×10 ft).

Tobacco plants (*Nicotiana affinis* 'Nicki' and *Lobelia* 'String of Pearls').

Mahonia japonica has long trusses of pale yellow flowers smelling of lily-of-the-valley in winter. (See page 82.)

Myrtle (*Myrtus communis*) is a large, evergreen shrub whose leaves and small, white, fluffy flowers, borne all summer, are both strongly scented.
Flowers Jul–Sept. Approx. height and spread after five years 1×1 m (3×3 ft); after ten years 2×2 m (6×6 ft).

Osmanthus delavayi has very sweetly scented, small, white flowers in spring. (See page 146.)

Mock orange (*Philadelphus* species) is an essential ingredient of any scented border. (See page 146.)

California tree poppy (*Romneya coulteri*). (See page 147.)

Roses in their shrub and bush forms are also a must for any scented border. Again there is a huge choice, but where space is at a premium look for those with additional qualities, such as a long flowering season and attractive foliage. Among the many outstanding varieties are the blush-white 'Margaret Merril', the pale pink 'City of London' and 'Bonica' and the dusky scarlet 'Fragrant Cloud'. Among the English roses 'Graham Thomas', 'Heritage' and 'Othello' all have good fragrance. (See page 147.)

Rosemary (*Rosmarinus officinalis*) has powerfully aromatic foliage. (See page 171.)

Sage (*Salvia officinalis*) in its variegated as well as its plain forms has strongly aromatic foliage. Ask any pig. (See page 175.)

Golden elder and golden cut-leaved elder (*Sambucus nigra* 'Aurea' and *S. racemosa* 'Plumosa Aurea') both have flat heads of white musk-scented flowers, used in home wine making for elderflower champagne. (See page 63.)

Cotton lavender (*Santolina*) in all its forms has very pungent foliage, sweet yet sharp at the same time. (See page 171.)

Christmas box (*Sarcococca humilis*) is grown largely for its vanilla-scented flowers in winter. (See page 63.)

Lilac (*Syringa*) in many of its forms has superbly sweet-scented flowers. (See page 148.)

Viburnum includes in its large and varied ranks many of the most sweetly scented shrubs of all. For winter scent *Viburnum farreri* and the smaller-growing *V.* × *bodnantense* (especially *V.b.* 'Dawn') are superb, as is the evergreen *V. tinus.* For spring fragrance look for the evergreen *V.* × *burkwoodii*, which can be in flower as early as January in a sheltered spot; *V. carlesii*, with pink-budded, white flowers smelling like pinks; and *V. juddii*, with exquisitely scented, pale pink flowers in April–May. (See page 150.)

HERBACEOUS PLANTS

Elephant's ears (*Bergenia cordifolia, B. crassifolia* and *B. schmidtii*) all have scented flowers in winter and early spring. (See page 70.)

Wallflowers (*Cheiranthus cheiri*) are usually grown as biennials (grown from seed one year, flowering the next, then dying), but in some sheltered areas they will survive longer. There are many varieties available, but the more compact, double-flowered Siberian wallflowers (*C.* × *allionii*) have the best perfume. The variety *C.c.* 'Harper Crewe' is believed to date from the reign of Elizabeth I and has small, double, yellow, sweetly scented flowers.
Flowers Mar–May. Approx. height and spread 40 × 30 cm (16 × 12 in).

Lily-of-the-valley (*Convallaria majalis*) does best in part shade, so plant it beneath shrubs. Sweet, lasting fragrance. (See page 87.)

Pinks (*Dianthus*), in many forms, have sweetly scented flowers. (See page 174.)

Burning bush (*Dictamnus albus*) is so called because it gives off a volatile oil when the seed heads are ripening which is inflammable. The dark green leaves smell of balsam when crushed and it also has very attractive white flowers in summer.
Flowers Jun–Aug. Approx. height and spread 80 × 40 cm (2½ ft × 16 in).

Sweet rocket (*Hesperis matronalis*) is a biennial which seeds itself so freely that once you have it you are never without it. During the daytime its pale mauve or white flowers have a faint violet scent, but in the evening it becomes much stronger like cloves.
Flowers Apr–May. Approx. height and spread 75×30 cm ($2\frac{1}{2} \times 1$ ft).

Lemon balm (*Melissa officinalis* 'Aurea') has lemon-scented leaves which are gold with a green central vein. It needs to be cut hard back in late spring to encourage bright new foliage and to prevent flowering, which makes the plant straggly.
Approx. height and spread 60×60 cm (2×2 ft).

Bergamot (*Monarda didyma*) has aromatic leaves and pink, red or white flowers.
Flowers Jun–Sept. Approx. height and spread 75×35 cm ($2\frac{1}{2} \times 1\frac{1}{4}$ ft).

Evening primrose in its biennial form *Oenothera biennis* has sweetly scented flowers, opening at dusk, as does the perennial *O. odorata*, though it's much harder to find. (See page 175.)

Russian sage (*Perovskia atriplicifolia*), as its name suggests, has leaves, stems and flowers that all smell of sage. (See page 170.)

Phlox (*Phlox paniculata*) has a strong fragrance. (See page 156.)

Primula has a few sweetly scented forms – some of the rarer ones like *Primula chionantha* and the most common form, *P. vulgaris*, the true primrose. (See page 73.)

Thyme (*Thymus* species). (See page 176.)

Verbena has surprisingly few scented forms. Look for *Verbena rigida*, which has violet-purple flowers all summer long, and the smaller *V. corymbosa*, with clusters of violet-blue flowers.
Flowers Jul–Sept. Approx. height and spread 40×30 cm (16×12 in).

ANNUALS
Half-hardy annuals to be bought as plants
All flowering June–September

Heliotrope or cherry pie (*Heliotropium arborescens*) has large clusters of deep violet-blue flowers with a heady, rather fruity scent – hence its common name. 'Marine' and 'Mini Marine' are good varieties, the latter a few inches shorter than the former.
Approx. height and spread 45–50×30 cm (16–18×12 in).

Stocks are a superbly scented family of showy spring- and summer-flowering cottage garden annuals and biennials in shades of white,

7. Rose 'Alberic Barbier'
and *Clematis viticella*
'Etoile Violette'

27. *Chamaecyparis
lawsoniana* 'Pottenii'

62. *Lilium regale*

4. *Lonicera
periclymenum*
'Serotina'

61. *Viola cornuta*

29. *Juniperus
squamata*
'Blue Star'

28. *Chamaecyparis
lawsoniana* 'Minima
Aurea'

60. *Penstemon*
'Garnet'

30. *Buddle
fallowiar
alba*

31. *Artemisia* 'Powis Castle'.

57. *Corylopsis pauciflora*

10. Rose 'Pink Perpetue' and Clematis *Jackmanii Superba*

56. *Viburnum juddii*

14. *Malus* 'Profusion'

62. *Lilium regale*

5. *Rosa bonica*

58. *Liriope muscari*

55. *Geranium nodosum*

17. *Mahonia* 'Charity'

yellow, pink, mauve, lavender and red. Ten-week stock (*Matthiola incana*) is a half-hardy annual, while Brompton stock (also *Matthiola incana*) is a biennial. Virginia stock (*Malcolmia maritima*) is an easily grown hardy annual with small flowers in white, pink or mauve, while night-scented stock (*Matthiola bicornis*) is a hardy annual with small, insignificant flowers, but its fragrance at night is superb – it is worth growing among the more attractive-looking stocks.

Approx. height and spread 30–50 cm (1–1½ ft).

Tobacco plants (*Nicotiana* species) are all scented, though the many coloured hybrids – with the exception of a mixture called 'Evening Fragrance' – are not as sweetly scented, particularly in the evenings, as the white *N. affinis*. If you can find it, the short-lived perennial *N. sylvestris*, which can reach almost 2 m (6 ft) in height, also has superb fragrance in the evening. It's easy to collect your own seed, so you can keep it going from year to year. (See page 160.)

Hardy annuals to be sown where they are to flower

Alyssum maritima in its white forms has a scent some people describe as like new-mown hay. (See page 160.)

Mignonette (*Reseda odorata*). (See page 162.)

Sweet peas (*Lathyrus odoratus*). (See page 163.)

Sweet William (*Dianthus barbatus*) has several biennial and annual forms which have a fragrance slightly reminiscent of cloves. Look for the biennial 'auricula-eyed' form, which has bi-coloured red or pink and white flowers, or one of the annual dwarf mixtures like 'Roundabout' or 'Wee Willie'.

Approx. height and spread 15–45 × 15–30 cm (6–18 in × 6–12 in).

BULBS

Ornamental onions, particularly the yellow *Allium moly* and the white *A. neapolitanum*. (See page 163.)

Belladonna lily (*Amaryllis belladonna*). (See page 178.)

Crocuses have a delicate scent that is best appreciated close to in window boxes or indoors. (See page 164.)

Summer hyacinth (*Galtonia candicans*) has a perfume which seems to develop once the flowers have been cut and taken indoors. (See page 164.)

Hyacinths do have a sweet, almost cloying perfume indoors, but outside it is largely lost. (See page 164.)

Lilies, especially the white *Lilium regale*, have a stunning fragrance on warm days that seems to intensify in the evening. (See page 164.)

Narcissi, represented by the white 'Cheerfulness', are an essential ingredient of the Queen's Maundy Thursday nosegay, an indication of how strong their fragrance is. Other good varieties for fragrance include the jonquil narcissi like 'Trevithian', 'Lintie', 'Suzy' and *Narcissus jonquilla odorus rugulosus plenus*, and the old 'Pheasant's Eye' with its white petals and red and gold 'eye'. (See page 165.)

Fragrant Plants for Dry Soil

The choice is not as large here as for moist soil, but it's possible to create a very attractive scented border provided that you add lots of organic matter before you plant and, having given the border a thorough drenching once you've planted it, mulch with a generous layer of the same. Quite a few plants will tolerate drier conditions once they've settled in than they will right at the start.

CLIMBERS

Jasmine (*Jasminum officinale*). (See page 136.)

Honeysuckle prefers a cool, moist soil, but some varieties will tolerate dry and chalky soils, like *Lonicera periclymenum* 'Belgica' and *L.p.* 'Serotina' and the goat-leaved honeysuckle, *L. caprifolium*, with creamy-white flowers in midsummer which are particularly fragrant at night. (See page 137.)

SHRUBS

Barberry (*Berberis stenophylla*) makes a large, impenetrable thicket of arching stems covered in deep green, evergreen leaves and, in late spring, scented gold flowers.
Flowers Apr–May. Approx. height and spread after five years 1.5 × 1.5 m (5 × 5 ft); after ten years 2 × 2 m (6 × 6 ft).

Buddleia. (See page 139.)

Wintersweet (*Chimonanthus praecox*). (See page 115.)

Mexican orange blossom (*Choisya ternata*). (See page 140.)

Blue spiraea (*Caryopteris incana* × *mongolica* 'Arthur Simmonds'). (See page 167.)

Moroccan broom (*Cytisus battandieri*). (See page 136.)

Broom (*Genista* species). (See page 142.)

Top: Pinks (*Dianthus* 'Doris').

Below right: There are many varieties of sweet peas in a wide range of colours, so be sure to choose a strongly scented one.

Below: Fragrant mauve and white sweet rocket (*Hesperis matronalis*) with the scented, pale yellow rose *Rosa cantabrigiensis*.

Mahonia japonica, except in very dry soil. (See page 82.)

Myrtle (*Myrtus communis*). (See page 117.)

Osmanthus delavayi. (See page 146.)

Russian sage (*Perovskia atriplicifolia*). (See page 170.)

Mock orange (*Philadelphus* species), provided plenty of organic matter is added when planting. (See page 146.)

Roses don't, in general, do well on this type of soil. One very attractive exception is *Rosa xanthina* 'Canary Bird', which makes a tall shrub with arching branches covered in fern-like foliage and, in May, produces masses of single, bright yellow flowers. Approx. height and spread 2 × 2 m (6 × 6 ft).

Rosemary (*Rosmarinus officinalis*). (See page 171.)

Sage (*Salvia officinalis*). (See page 175.)

Golden elder (*Sambucus nigra* 'Aurea'). (See page 63.)

Above: Very fragrant regale lilies (*Lilium regale*), growing here with baby's breath (*Gypsophila paniculata*) and alstroemeria, are among the easiest lilies to grow.

Left: Mint, golden balm and chives, growing together in a herb border, demonstrate that herbs are highly ornamental as well as useful.

Spanish broom (*Spartium junceum*). (See page 171.)

Lilac (*Syringa* species). (See page 148.)

HERBACEOUS PLANTS
Elephant's ears (*Bergenia* species). (See page 70.)

Wallflowers (*Cheiranthus cheiri*). (See page 118.)

Lily-of-the-valley (*Convallaria majalis*) in the shade of shrubs. (See page 87.)

Pinks (*Dianthus* species. (See page 174.)

Burning bush (*Dictamnus albus*). (See page 118.)

Lemon balm (*Melissa officinalis* 'Aurea'). (See page 119.)

Evening primrose (*Oenothera* species). (See page 175.)

Bouncing Bette (*Saponaria ocymoides*). (See page 176.)

Thyme (*Thymus* species. (See page 176.)

ANNUALS
Few scented annuals really like dry soil, but the following are worth trying, if you enrich the soil with additional organic matter first.

Heliotrope or cherry pie (*Heliotropium arborescens*). (See page 119.)

Virginia stock (*Malcolmia maritima*). (See page 122.)

Tobacco plants (*Nicotiana* species). (See page 160.)

Mignonette (*Reseda odorata*). (See page 162.)

Ten-week, Brompton and night-scented stocks (*Matthiola incana* and *M. bicornis*). (See page 122.)

BULBS
Ornamental onions (*Allium* species). (See page 163.)

Belladonna lily (*Amaryllis belladonna*). (See page 178.)

Summer hyacinth (*Galtonia candicans*). (See page 164.)

Lily (*Lilium regale*). (See page 164.)

Fragrant Plants for Heavy Clay Soil

A particularly short list, this one, apart from quite a reasonable selection of shrubs, but you can still make a scented border with a little padding from non-scented herbaceous plants, annuals and bulbs. See pages 179–82 for those that will cope with a sunny site and heavy clay.

TREES
Laburnum (*Laburnum × watereri* 'Vossii'). (See page 40.)

Ornamental crab (*Malus floribunda* and *M. hupehensis*). (See page 40.)

SHRUBS
Barberry (*Berberis stenophylla*). (See page 139.)

Mexican orange blossom (*Choisya ternata*). (See page 140.)

Chinese witch hazel (*Hamamelis mollis*). (See page 61.)

Mahonia japonica. (See page 82.)

Osmanthus delavayi. (See page 146.)

Mock orange (*Philadelphus* species). (See page 146.)

Roses. (See page 147.)

Golden elder (*Sambucus nigra* 'Aurea'). (See page 63.)

Viburnum × bodnantense, V. × burkwoodii, V. tinus. (See page 150.)

HERBACEOUS PLANTS, ANNUALS AND BULBS
Apart from day lilies (*Hemerocallis* species), some of which are scented, there are few fragrant plants that will grow in heavy clay soil in a sunny position.

Planting Plan for a Dry, West-facing Border
(See illus. on pages 128–9.)

The months when the flowers are most fragrant are given after the notes on each plant unless it is grown mainly for its foliage.

32. *Viburnum × burkwoodii*

3. *Lilium regale*

34. Bronze fennel

31. *Loni*
'Early Du

1. *Philadelphus*
'Belle Etoile'

22. *Phlox*
paniculata

21. *Cy*
keven

35. *Buddleia*
fallowiana
'Lochinch'

23. *Rosemarinus*
officinalis

9. *Cheiranthis cheiri*
'Harpur Crewe'

8. *Salvia officinalis* 'Purpurescans'

2. *Allium*
albopilosu

6. *Syringa microphylla* 'Superba'

7. *Lavandula*
angustifolia
'Hidcote'

10. *Marjoram*
'Aurea'

11. Chives
(*Allium*
schoenoprasum

5. *Lippia citriodora*

2. *Allium albopilosum*

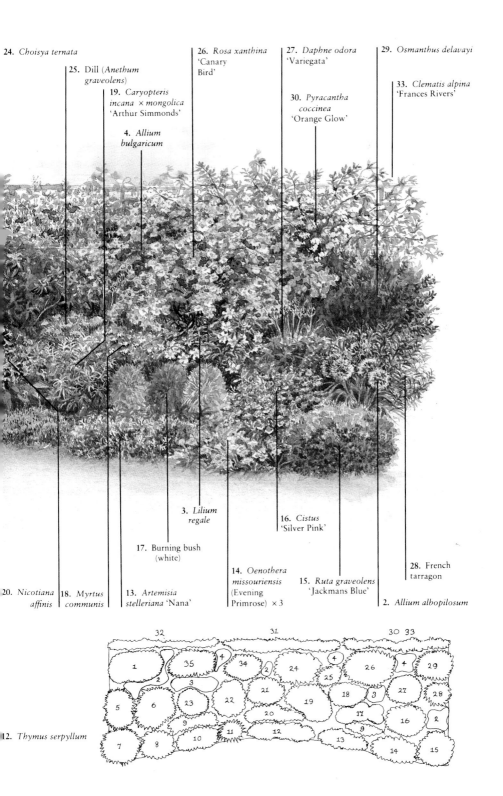

24. *Choisya ternata*

25. Dill (*Anethum graveolens*)

19. *Caryopteris incana* × *mongolica* 'Arthur Simmonds'

4. *Allium bulgaricum*

26. *Rosa xanthina* 'Canary Bird'

27. *Daphne odora* 'Variegata'

30. *Pyracantha coccinea* 'Orange Glow'

29. *Osmanthus delavayi*

33. *Clematis alpina* 'Frances Rivers'

3. *Lilium regale*

16. *Cistus* 'Silver Pink'

17. Burning bush (white)

14. *Oenothera missouriensis* (Evening Primrose) × 3

15. *Ruta graveolens* 'Jackmans Blue'

28. French tarragon

20. *Nicotiana affinis*

18. *Myrtus communis*

13. *Artemisia stelleriana* 'Nana'

2. *Allium albopilosum*

12. *Thymus serpyllum*

CLIMBERS
Allow 3 m (10 ft) for each plant.

1 *Viburnum × burkwoodii* trained as wall shrub. Evergreen. March–May. (See pages 118, 150.)

2, 3 Early and late Dutch honeysuckle (*Lonicera periclymenum* 'Belgica' and *L.p.* 'Serotina') grown together. May–September. (See page 137.)

4 Firethorn (*Pyracantha coccinea* 'Orange Glow'). Evergreen. Bright orange berries in winter. Scented flowers June. (See page 62.) Host to:

5 *Clematis alpina* 'Frances Rives'. Not scented, but very pretty blue and white flowers in April–May. (See page 135.)

SHRUBS
A Mock orange (*Philadelphus* 'Belle Etoile'). June–July. (See page 146.)

B *Buddleia fallowiana* 'Lochinch'. July–August. (See page 139.)

C 3 × bronze fennel (*Foeniculum vulgare purpureum*). Aromatic foliage – good as a flavouring in fish dishes. (See page 174.)

D Mexican orange blossom (*Choisya ternata*). Evergreen, pungent foliage. April–June and often again in September. (See page 140.)

E *Rosa xanthina* 'Canary Bird'. May–June. (See page 125.)

F *Osmanthus delavayi*. April. (See page 146.)

PERENNIALS AND SMALL SHRUBS
a Lemon verbena (*Lippia citriodora*). (See page 117.)

b Littleleaf lilac (*Syringa microphylla* 'Superba'). May–June and again in September. (See page 148.)

c *Rosmarinus officinalis*. (See page 171.)

c(i) 3 × *Phlox paniculata* 'White Admiral'. (See page 156.)

d Broom (*Cytisus kewensis*). Cream, scented flowers. May–June. (See page 142.)

e Blue spiraea (*Caryopteris incana × mongolica* 'Arthur Simmonds'). Aromatic foliage. (See page 167.)

e(i) 3 × dill (*Anethum graveolens*). Feathery, aromatic, green leaves, 1 m (3 ft). Good as a flavouring with fish and in pickles.
Approx. height and spread 1 m × 30 cm (3 ft × 9–12 in).

f Myrtle (*Myrtus communis*). Aromatic, evergreen leaves. July–September. (See page 117.)

g Winter daphne (*Daphne odora* 'Variegata'). Variegated evergreen. February–March. (See pages 115, 142.)

h 3 × French tarragon (*Artemisia dracunculus*). Aromatic foliage. Approx. height and spread 45 × 30 cm (1½ft × 1 ft).

i Lavender (*Lavandula angustifolia* 'Hidcote'). (See page 170.)

j Sweet rocket (*Hesperis matronalis*). April–June. (See page 119.)

k Purple-leafed sage (*Salvia officinalis* 'Purpurascens'). The colour doesn't affect the flavour of the leaves. (See page 175.)

l Golden marjoram (*Origanum aureum*). Aromatic foliage. Approx. height and spread 60 × 30 cm (2 ft × 1 ft).

m Chives (*Allium schoenoprasum*). Attractive pink flowers, as well as onion-flavoured foliage. A useful 'vertical' plant among the horizontals.

n Thyme (*Thymus serpyllum*). Aromatic foliage. (See page 176.)

o *Artemisia stelleriana* 'Nana'. A dwarf ornamental silver artemisia. Aromatic, non-edible foliage. (See page 151.)

p Perennial wallflower (*Cheiranthis cheiri* 'Harper Crewe'). March–May. (See page 118.)

q Burning bush (*Dictamnus fraxinella* 'Alba'). June–August. (See page 118.)

r Evening primrose (*Oenothera missouriensis*). June–September. (See page 175.)

s Rock rose (*Cistus* 'Silver Pink'). June–July. (See page 169.)

t Rue (*Ruta graveolens* 'Jackman's Blue'). Superb heads of tiny, blue-green bitter-tasting leaves. Cut back hard in spring to ensure the best new foliage.
Approx. height and spread 60 × 80 cm (2 × 2½ ft).

u Tobacco plant (*Nicotiana affine*). June–September. (See page 160.)

BULBS

Ornamental onions (*Allium* species). Tall ones like *A. bulgaricum* and *A. albopilosum* at the back of the borders. (See page 163.)

Lily (*Lilium regale*). July. (See page 164.)

CHAPTER SEVEN

South-facing borders

In many ways a south-facing border which gets sun all day is the easiest of all to plant because there are so many wonderful climbers, shrubs, herbaceous plants, annuals and bulbs which simply revel in a sunny spot. If there is a problem with south-facing borders it's that the range of suitable plants is so vast that, like a child given *carte blanche* in a sweet shop, you really are spoilt for choice! The temptation to try to cram too much in is very strong, and certainly one way of resisting it is to choose a theme for your border and stick to that. It could be a colour scheme – hot reds, oranges and golds, say – or a particular type of plant – traditional cottage garden plants, for example. Alternatively, you could choose one family of plants as the backbone of your border – small shrub roses, for intance, or the lovely 'English' roses (combining the beauty and perfume of old roses with the compactness, repeat-flowering and vigour of new hybrids) – and then select the other plants to fit in with them. You could choose tall plants to give the border height and form a background for the roses – plants like blue- or white-flowered campanulas, say, regale lilies, the annual white and pink lavateras, verbascums such as the lovely soft yellow 'Gainsborough', the striking, feathery, bronze fennel (*Foeniculum vulgare purpureum*) and silvery artemisia. You could then add some lower-growing, mound-forming subjects such as cotton lavender (*Santolina chamaecyparissus*) and, indeed, lavender itself, small hebes like *Hebe pinguifolia* 'Pagei', hardy geraniums such as the widely available 'Johnson's Blue', herbs like sage, gold and silver thymes, marjoram ... it's still easy to get carried away, even when you have imposed some sort of scheme upon yourself!

Again, there are really two main types of sunny border. First there are those with moisture-retentive but reasonably well-drained soil – which includes not only the elusive medium loam, but also soils of a moderate clay content whose drainage has been improved with organic matter and grit, and moderately sandy and even limy soils whose moisture-retaining qualities have been boosted with

A romantic garden in pastel colours – the white sea kale (*Crambe cordifolia*) and mock orange (*Philadelphus*) and the blue delphiniums against a background of pale pink climbing roses.

large amounts of organic matter. Obviously, if you have a limy soil, you still won't be able to grow acid-loving plants, but this time, as well as many of the plants suitable for average soils, you'll also be able to grow some beautiful specimens that do best on lime, like lilac, mock orange, the lovely silver-leafed, blue-flowered *Caryopteris incana*, the long-flowering *Coronilla glauca* with its mass of yellow pea flowers, and the fragrant, winter-flowering wintersweet (*Chimonanthus praecox*).

The other sort of sunny border is the one with a thin, dry soil. Certainly, adding lots of organic matter can help its ability to retain water a little, but it will still be a dry soil. One answer would be to choose plants that need regular watering and to spend a great deal of time in the garden with the hose. But that's the gardening equivalent of washing-up and besides, if we ever get another hot, dry summer, the use of hosepipes will be one of the first things to be banned. And what with privatisation and metering on the way, watering the garden will be a very expensive operation. The best solution, again, is to choose plants that actually flourish in the conditions you're offering – in this instance, drought! – but we'll return to these later.

Acid-loving Plants

SHRUBS

Winter hazel (*Corylopsis pauciflora*), like its relative, witch hazel, has sweetly scented, yellow flowers on bare stems, though in this case in spring rather than in winter. The young foliage, when it does appear, is tinged with pink.
Approx. height and spread after five years 1 × 1 m (3 × 3 ft); after ten years 2 × 2 m (6 × 6 ft).

Heather (*Calluna vulgaris*) which flowers in the summer, between June and October, is a lime hater and needs an acid soil to do well. It comes in a range of colours – flowers in white, pink, red and purple and foliage in green, gold, grey, orange and, in the case of *C.v.* 'Winter Chocolate', chocolate brown in winter. A number of plants grouped together quickly make an attractive carpet. Incidentally, you should ignore the advice still given by some garden centres that on a limy soil you can dig a large hole, fill it with peaty soil and plant acid lovers in that. This is not successful, for no matter how large the hole, it's only a matter of time before limy water from the surrounding soil creeps in and turns your temporarily acid soil alkaline. If you don't have an acid soil and want to grow heathers, grow the winter-flowering kind (*Erica carnea*) which comes in as wide a range of flower and foliage colour, but which is happy on neutral and slightly limy soils.
Approx. height and spread after five and ten years 5–50 cm × 30 cm (2–18 in × 12 in).

Sweetspire (*Itea ilicifolia*), a medium-sized, evergreen shrub with holly-like leaves and fragrant, greenish-white flowers, closely packed in tassels rather like catkins, can be grown either free-standing or trained against a warm wall.
Approx. height and spread after five years 1 × 1 m (3 × 3 ft); after ten years 2 × 2 m (6 × 6 ft).

Calico bush (*Kalmia latifolia*) is rather like members of the rhododendron family in appearance, with large, glossy green, oval leaves which provide an ideal backdrop for the clusters of rose-pink, cup-shaped flowers in early summer. It will tolerate a little shade but does best in full sun.
Approx. height and spread after five years 1.5 × 1.5 m (5 × 5 ft); after ten years 2 × 2 m (6 × 6 ft).

Lithospermum diffusum is a small, evergreen, carpeting shrub with flowers of the most beautiful vivid gentian blue between May and August. The best variety is *L.d.* 'Grace Ward', which grows more vigorously and has flowers of an even more intense blue, but it's not as widely available as *L.d.* 'Heavenly Blue', which itself is such a stunning plant that it is no real hardship! A light clipping-over after flowering will make it grow more densely.

Approx. height and spread after five years 15 × 30 cm (6 × 12 in); after ten years 15 × 50 cm (6 × 18 in).

Moist Soil

CLIMBERS

Actinidia kolomikta is a superb twining foliage plant for a sunny wall or fence. It has large, heart-shaped leaves that start out green but quickly assume splashes of cream and pink on the lower portion which are so bold that you might think the Queen of Hearts' gardeners had been busy with their paint brushes.

Approx. height and spread after five years 3–4 m (10–13 ft).

Trumpet vine (*Campsis radicans*) needs a well-protected, sunny wall to do well, but its dramatic, large, orange-red, trumpet flowers, produced from August to October, make it worth taking the chance. It also has attractive, lush green foliage, not unlike that of wisteria.

Approx. height and spread after five years 4–5 m (13–16 ft).

Clematis, many of which like their heads in the sun and their roots in moist, shady, preferably limy soil, include so many different varieties that it's possible to have one in flower practically the whole year round. In winter there's the evergreen fern-leafed clematis (*Clematis balearica*) whose very delicate-looking foliage is tinged with bronze when the creamy-white, bell-shaped flowers appear. To follow on in spring there is *C. alpina*, with blue and white or pink nodding flowers, and in late spring/early summer *C. macropetala*, similar to *C. alpina* though its pink, blue or white flowers are semi-double and larger. (*C. montana* flowers at this time, but it is so vigorous that you really ought to think twice about planting it in a very small garden). Throughout the summer there are any number of large-flowered hybrids, though the pale pink and mauve varieties, like 'Nelly Moser' and 'Barbara Jackman', are better out of full sun since it causes their flowers to fade. In late summer there is *C. viticella*, with small single or double white, wine-red or rich purple flowers, or *C. orientalis*, the 'orange peel' clematis, which has grey-green foliage and nodding, yellow, cup-shaped flowers in September/October, followed by fluffy silvery seedheads that last into the winter. Since all large-flowered hybrids and many of the species (except *C. alpina*, *C. macropetala*, *C. orientalis*) need hard pruning each year to avoid getting bare, woody stems devoid of any flowers, it's useful to know how much growth they'll make in one season.

Approx. height and spread in one season – large-flowered hybrids 2–5 m (6–16 ft); small-flowered species 3–7 m (10–23 ft).

The extraordinary coloration of *Actinidia kolomikta* is at its best in full sun.

Moroccan broom (*Cytisus battandieri*) is a fast-growing wall shrub which has attractive, large, silvery leaves and plumes of bright yellow flowers that smell of sweet, ripe pineapple. It dislikes both very acid and very alkaline soils, but will grow happily in ordinary and even poor, dry soils.

Approx. height and spread after five years 4.5×2 m (14×6 ft); after ten years 6.5×4 m (22×13 ft).

Chilean glory flower (*Eccremocarpus scaber*), which produces masses of orange-red, tubular flowers from August to October, is only completely hardy in the mildest areas of the country. Everywhere else it will get cut down to the ground by the first hard frost, but don't despair: pile some strawy manure or even peat over the roots to protect them through the cold season and after all but the hardest winters it will shoot again in spring. Alternatively, if you collect seed in the autumn, it's very easy to raise new plants that way in the spring.

Approx. height and spread in one season 3 m + (10 ft +).

Jasmine (*Jasminum officinale*) produces small, white flowers with one of the strongest, sweetest fragrances of all, particularly in the evening, which makes it an especially good choice for a west-facing wall (see page 114). It's a twining plant, and a very untidy

grower, so you'll need to treat it with a firm hand if it is on a wall or fence. Better still, grow it over an arch, arbour or even a shed, where its untidiness won't matter. There is a pink-flowered variety, *J.o. stephanense*, and two lovely ones with variegated leaves, *J.o.* 'Aureovariegatum' with pale yellow variegated leaves and *J.o.* 'Argenteovariegatum' with cream variegated leaves, though you'd probably find the latter only in a specialist nursery. Approx. height and spread after ten years 9 m (30 ft).

Clematis macropetala.

Honeysuckle (*Lonicera* species), like clematis, is happiest with its head in the sun and its roots in the shade, so either plant shrubs in front of the honeysuckle to provide shade, or mulch the roots well with a deep layer of organic matter. For a long flowering period, plant both. *L. periclymenum* 'Belgica', the early Dutch honeysuckle, which in early summer and often again in early autumn has sweetly scented, pale rose-purple, tubular flowers that are yellow within, and *L.p.* 'Serotina', the late Dutch honeysuckle, whose flowers, darker red outside and paler yellow inside are produced from midsummer to mid-autumn. For brighter flowers, though without any scent, try *L.* × *brownii* 'Fuchsoides', which has brilliant orange-scarlet flowers in late spring and again in late summer. Approx. height and spread 4.5–6 m (15–20 ft).

Passionflower (*Passiflora caerulea*), provided with a warm, sheltered wall or fence, will produce a succession of its large, intriguing flowers – white petals with a central ring of fine purple growths in which are the three styles and five anthers, said to symbolise the three nails and five wounds of the Crucifixion that give the plant its common name. The individual flowers are not long-lived, but so many of them are produced between June and September that it doesn't matter. In mild areas it is almost evergreen, but a really hard frost will cut the growth to the ground. If you protect the roots as described for the Chilean glory flower's, though, after all but the coldest winters it should produce new growth in spring.
Approx. height and spread (in mild areas) 4 × 3 m (13 × 10 ft).

Roses, in their climbing and rambling forms, are another family that leave you spoilt for choice, both in colour and shape of flower – from the simple, almost flat, creamy-yellow flowers of 'Mermaid' to the elaborate, many-petalled, deep cerise-pink flowers of the thornless 'Zéphirine Drouhin'. Go for a repeat-flowering variety that will flower more or less non-stop from June to October, or even later in a mild autumn, rather than one which flowers for only a few weeks in June. First-class varieties include the pinky-apricot 'Compassion', the deep rose-pink 'Aloha', the deep yellow 'Golden Showers', the white 'Climbing Iceburg', the pearly, blush-pink 'New Dawn', 'Paul's Scarlet Climber' and 'Pink Perpétue', with clusters of double, carmine-pink flowers.
Approx. final height depending on variety 2.5–4 m (8–13 ft).

Chilean potato tree (*Solanum crispum*) is a very mundane name for an extremely pretty climber, though, to be fair, it is related to the common-or-garden potato. Given a warm, sheltered wall or fence, and a well-drained soil, it will produce rounded clusters of small, mauve flowers with prominent, bright yellow stamens in abundance from June to October. It's a wall shrub, not a climber, so will need supporting, either on horizontal wires or, better still, on chicken wire (see page 18). Its long stems are sometimes killed by frosts in cold areas, but it takes a really severe winter to kill the plant altogether. Usually it starts into growth again the following spring. It has a beautiful but even more tender relative, *S. jasminoides* 'Album', which produces clusters of pure white flowers with the same prominent gold stamens. If you live in a particularly sheltered spot, try growing it – it's well worth the gamble.
Approx. height after five years (if not cut back by frosts) 5–6 m (16–20 ft).

Wisteria is one of the most stunning climbing plants, with its huge trusses of violet-blue flowers hanging down in late spring and early summer. It does require quite careful pruning of its twining growths in late summer and again in winter if it is to produce flowers, and even so it can take five years or more for it to bloom for the first time. There is also a white variety, *Wisteria sinensis* 'Alba', while the much less vigorous *W. floribunda* 'Macrobotrys' has trusses of lilac-blue flowers almost 1 m (3 ft) long!

Approx. height and spread after ten years 20 m + (66 ft +); *W.f.* 'Macrobotrys' 9 m (30 ft).

SHRUBS

Southernwood (*Artemisia abrotanum*) has sweetly aromatic, very finely divided, grey-green leaves and small, bobbly flowers in early summer. It has a more beautiful relative, *A. arborescens*, with a mass of filigree silver leaves, but sadly this isn't as hardy and a really cold winter will kill it off. Unless you're a gambler, one of the tall perennial artemisias (see page 151) is a safer bet.

Approx. height and spread after five years 80 × 80 cm ($2\frac{1}{2} \times 2\frac{1}{2}$ft); after ten years 80 cm × 1.2 m ($2\frac{1}{2} \times 4$ ft).

Barberry (*Berberis thunbergii*), in its purple-, red- and pink-leafed forms, needs full sun to give of its best. Apart from striking foliage, they also have flowers in spring, berries in autumn and, in most cases, lovely autumn colour. There are several different shapes. One of the best stiff, upright varieties is *B.t.* 'Helmond Pillar', with deep purple leaves, while for something tall but with gracefully arching branches look for the brilliant wine-red *B.t.* 'Red Chief'. For a low, semi-spreading shrub, *B.t.* 'Dart's Red Lady', which has deep purple leaves which turn a vivid fiery red in autumn, is hard to beat. The little, bun-shaped *B.t.* 'Bagatelle', which reaches no more than 30 cm (1 ft) in height, is ideal in a group for the front of a border.

Approx. height and spread after five years 1 m × 60 cm (3 × 2 ft); after ten years 1.8 × 1.5 ($5\frac{1}{2} \times 5$ ft).

Butterfly bush (*Buddleia davidii*) acts like a magnet for butterflies in any garden and is also an attractive summer-flowering shrub in its own right. There are many excellent named varieties from which to choose, with flowers in a range of colours from white to almost black (*B.d.* 'Black Night'), but where space is limited smaller-growing varieties, like *B.d.* 'Nanho Alba' and 'Nanho Purple', are a good choice. Two lovely relatives well worth considering are *B. fallowiana* 'Alba', which has sweetly scented, pure white flowers with an orange eye and foliage that's silver-white when young fading to a very pale grey, and *B.* × 'Lochinch', with lavender-blue flowers, again with an orange eye, and similar silvery-grey foliage. All buddleias benefit from cutting back hard every year or two, otherwise they become straggly and produce smaller flowers.

Approx. height and spread after five years 1.5–2.5 m × 1.5–2.5 m (5–8 ft × 5–8 ft); after ten years (if unpruned) 2–3.5 m × 2–3.5 m (6–12 ft × 6–12 ft).

Carpenteria californica is an evergreen, summer-flowering shrub for a sunny wall in a sheltered garden. It has large, saucer-shaped, white flowers and long, glossy, bright green leaves. A really cold winter will cut it back to the ground, and though it will usually produce new growth in the spring, it will take a couple of years before it flowers again.
Flowers Jun–Jul. Approx. height and spread after five years 1×1 m (3×3 ft); after ten years 1.5×1.5 m (5×5 ft).

Californian lilac (*Ceanothus* species), when it's smothered with bright blue thimbles of flowers in early summer, is a startling sight. There are both evergreen and deciduous kinds, and some can eventually make very large shrubs indeed, though the evergreen varieties are not totally hardy in colder areas. Among the best deciduous varieties are C. 'Gloire de Versailles', with powder-blue flowers in midsummer, and the much deeper blue C. 'Topaz'. Among the hardiest and/or smallest-growing evergreen varieties are C. *impressus*, with distinctive, small, glossy green leaves, often curled at the edges, and masses of small, deep blue flowers in late spring, which doesn't grow to much more than 1.3–1.5 m (4–5 ft) in height and spread; and C. *thyrsiflorus repens* 'Creeping Blue Blossom', which very quickly forms a mound of dense, evergreen foliage no more than 1 m (3 ft) in height and is smothered in mid-blue blossom in May.
Approx. height and spread after five years 1×1.2 m (3×4 ft); after ten years 1.3×1.5 m (4×5 ft); C. *thyrsiflorus repens* after ten years 1×2.5 m (3×8 ft).

Ceratostigma willmottianum produces masses of deep blue, saucer-shaped flowers from August to the first autumn frosts. If the stems aren't cut back to the ground by a hard frost, prune them back in spring to stop the shrub becoming leggy and to encourage flowering. C. *plumbaginoides*, with bright blue flowers, grows to only about a quarter of the size, making it a useful ground-cover plant.
Approx. height and spread after five years (unpruned) 60×60 cm (2×2 ft); after ten years 1×1 m (3×3 ft).

Mexican orange blossom (*Choisya ternata*), with its glossy, aromatic, evergreen leaves and profusion of small, white, scented flowers in summer and often again in autumn, will grow in shade as well as full sun, though it flowers more freely in sun. It forms a large, rounded bush, but can be pruned to keep it within the allotted space. There is also a new golden variety, C.t. 'Sundance', which reaches just over half its parent's height and is more tender. It dislikes deep shade and some people do not find the flowers as fragrant.
Approx. height and spread after five years 1×1.2 m (3×4 ft); after ten years 2×1.8 m ($6 \times 5\frac{1}{2}$ ft).

The repeat-flowering, fragrant climbing rose 'Pink Perpétue'.

Smoke bush (*Cotinus coggygria*) gets its common name from the clouds of tiny flowers that cover it all summer, turning a smoky grey in the autumn. The purple-leafed varieties, like *C.c.* 'Royal Purple' or 'Notcutt's Variety', are the most stunning, with wine-red foliage in spring and summer, and superb autumn colour too, as well as the clouds of 'smoky' flowers. You can cut it hard back each spring, as Rosemary Verey does, to produce bigger, brighter leaves, but if you do, you lose the flowers, which are produced on the previous season's wood.

Approx. height and spread after five years 1.5 × 1.5 m (5 × 5 ft); after ten years 3 × 3 m (10 × 10 ft).

Cotoneaster is another large family with members of all shapes and sizes, deciduous and evergreen, some of which will thrive in practically every garden situation. In a small garden, some of the ground-covering, small-leafed evergreens, which can cope with full sun and shade, are ideal. Look for *Cotoneaster dammeri* ('Coral Beauty' is a particularly good form), with white flowers in summer followed by sealing-wax-red berries. The slow-growing *C. micro-*

phyllus, good for covering a bank or for growing over a wall, has masses of tiny, grey-green leaves and dark red fruits in autumn and forms a low mound, rather than growing flat like *C. dammeri*.
Approx. height and spread after five years 30–50 cm × 1.2 m (12–18 in × 4 ft); after ten years 30–60 cm × 2 m (1–2 ft × 6 ft).

Broom (*Cytisus* species) also comes in many different shapes and sizes, and though most people think of them as having yellow flowers, in fact they come in a range of colours from cream through pink and mauve to rich red and maroon. Among the excellent low-growing varieties, look for *Cytisus kewensis*, with a mass of cream flowers in May; *C. × beanii*, with rich yellow flowers at the same time; and *C. purpureus*, with lovely soft mauve-pink flowers. Among the taller blooms notable varieties are *C. scoparius* 'Lena', which has superb ruby red and pale yellow flowers, and the much taller *C. × praecox* 'Allgold', which is a blaze of golden yellow flowers in spring.
Approx. height and spread after five years – low-growing species 50 × 80 cm ($1\frac{1}{2}$ × $2\frac{1}{2}$ ft); taller-growing species 60 × 80 cm (2 × $2\frac{1}{2}$ ft); after ten years 50 cm × 1.2 m ($1\frac{1}{2}$ × 4 ft) and 1.2 × 2 m (4 × 6 ft) respectively.

Daphne is another large family, and includes two of the best winter-flowering shrubs: *Daphne mezereum*, which produces clusters of sweetly scented, purple-red or white flowers on bare wood in February and March, while the small pink and white flowers of *D. odora* are even more fragrant. They do best in deep, rich, moist soil, but will tolerate some lime. The evergreen native daphne, *D. laureola*, which has yellow flowers in early spring, dislikes full sun and does best in medium shade.
Approx. height and spread after five years 60 × 60 cm (2 × 2 ft); after ten years 80 × 80 cm ($2\frac{1}{2}$ × $2\frac{1}{2}$ ft).

Winter-flowering heather (*Erica carnea*), unlike its summer flowering relative, doesn't need an acid soil. (See page 98.)

Escallonia is a valuable, summer-flowering, evergreen shrub, though in a really cold winter it may lose its leaves and start into growth again in spring, taking perhaps two or three years to regain its former size. It has masses of small flowers in a range of colours from white through many shades of pink to rich red. Good varieties include *Escallonia* 'Donard Seedling', with very pale pink flowers; *E.* 'Donard Star', with deep green foliage and rose-pink flowers; the taller-than-average *E.* 'Iveyi', with very glossy, very dark green leaves and large, pure white flowers; and *E.* 'Peach Blossom', with soft peachy-pink flowers.
Approx. height and spread after five years 1.5 × 1.5 m (4 × 4 ft); after ten years 2 × 1.8 m (6 × $5\frac{1}{2}$ ft).

Spindle (*Euonymus fortunei*) will grow in full sun as well as in shade. (See page 79.)

Fremontodendron californicum makes a large, stunning, wall shrub in a sunny, sheltered spot, with big, lobed, green-grey leaves covered in down, and large, buttercup-yellow flowers throughout the summer. It is susceptible to frost in the first few years, but once established is pretty hardy. It will also tolerate high alkalinity.
Approx. height and spread after five years 3×3 m (10×10 ft); after ten years 5×5 m (16×16 ft).

Chinese witch hazel (*Hamamelis mollis*) will also grow in full sun as well as in shade. (See page 61.)

Shrubby veronicas (*Hebe* species), mostly from New Zealand, include many very useful flowering evergreen shrubs. Some of the smaller ones are worth growing for their foliage alone – the ground-covering, blue-grey *Hebe pinguifolia* 'Pagei', for example, and the mound-forming *H. albicans*, with small, densely packed, elliptical, grey-green leaves. They won't reach much more than 50 cm $\times 1$ m ($1\frac{1}{2} \times 3$ ft) in ten years, they are both hardy and have stubby spikes of white flowers from early summer onwards. Of the larger hebes, *H.* 'Midsummer Beauty', *H.* × *franciscana* 'Blue Gem' and *H.* 'Autumn Glory', which all have mauve or lavender-blue flowers at various times throughout the summer, and the pink-flowered *H.* 'Great Orme' are all good. There are lovely variegated varieties too, like *H.* × *andersonii* 'Variegata', but they are even less hardy than their plainer relatives and won't survive a very cold winter.
Approx. height and spread after five years 1×1 m (3×3 ft); after ten years 1.5×1.5 m (5×5 ft).

Rose of Sharon (*Hypericum calycinum*) is best avoided unless you have acres to fill, since it becomes very clear after a season or two that world domination is its ultimate goal! A far better bet is *H. patulum* 'Hidcote', which has shallow, saucer-shaped, golden-yellow flowers all summer long and is semi-evergreen.
Approx. height and spread after five years 60×60 m (2×2 ft); after ten years 1×1 m (3×3 ft).

Beauty bush (*Kolkwitzia amabilis*) has lovely, soft pink, bell-shaped flowers from late spring to midsummer on wood at least three years old. It does best in full sun, although Rosemary Verey has a large specimen trained against a north-facing wall. There's a variety called 'Pink Cloud' which has larger flowers and starts producing them earlier in life than its parent.
Approx. height and spread after five years 1.5×1.5 m (5×5 ft); after ten years 2.5×2.5 m (8×8 ft).

13. *Sorbus
    cashmiriana*

25. *Philadelphus
    coronarius* 'Aureus'

6. *Solanum crispum*
   'Glasnevin'

38. *Allium
    schoenoprasum*
    'Forescate'

36. Lupin 'Russell
    Hybrids'

37. *Alstromeria*
    'Princess'

32. Delphinium hybrids

26. *Cotinus coggygria*
    'Atropurpurea'

11. Rose 'Mermaid'

31. *Artemisia* 'Powis
    Castle'.

34. *Stachys olympicum*
    'Primrose Heron'

33. *Anthemis
    cupaniana*

35. *Coreopsis
    verticillata*
    'Moonbeam'

Tree mallow (*Lavatera olbia* 'Rosea') is a quick-growing, upright, long-flowering shrub, with large, silvery-pink flowers. It's good for the back of the border. Hard pruning in spring encourages better flowering. There is an attractive new variety, *L.* 'Barnsley', which has blush-white flowers with a red centre.
Approx. height and spread after five years 2.5×2 m (8×6 ft); after ten years 3×3 m (10×10 ft).

Magnolias are among the most beautiful flowering shrubs and trees, but most are much too large for a small garden. An exception is *Magnolia stellata*, which is covered in white, star-shaped flowers with long, slender petals in April and May, before the leaves appear. *M.s.* 'Royal Star' has larger flowers which appear a little later.
Approx. height and spread after five years 80 cm $\times$ 1 m ($2\frac{1}{2} \times 3$ ft); after ten years 1.5×2 m (5×6 ft).

Osmanthus delavayi is a useful evergreen shrub with small leaves and superbly scented, small, white flowers in spring – ideal for cutting and taking indoors. It's happy in most soils, including chalk.
Approx. height and spread after five years 2×2 m (6×6 ft); after ten years 3×3 m (10×10 ft).

Mock orange (*Philadelphus* species) gets its common name from its sweet-scented white flowers, borne in profusion in June and July. Again there are a number of good varieties, though those that grow to 3 m + (10 ft +) are not ideal for small gardens. Among the best small varieties are 'Aureus', 'Belle Etoile', which forms an arching shrub covered in superbly scented, large, single, white flowers, and the smallest of all, 'Manteau d'Hermine', whose twiggy branches are smothered in creamy-white, double flowers.
Approx. height and spread after five years 80 cm–1 m $\times$ 80 cm–1 m ($2\frac{1}{2}$–3 ft $\times$ $2\frac{1}{2}$–3 ft); after ten years 1–1.5×1–1.5 m (3–5 ft $\times$ 3–5 ft).

Potentillas (*Potentilla fruticosa*) make small to medium-sized, rounded bushes which carry their small, pretty, open-faced flowers for months on end. There are many good varieties from which to choose, some well-established like the yellow-flowered 'Katherine Dykes', 'Elizabeth' and 'Goldfinger'; the pure white-flowered 'Abbotswood', with soft grey foliage; the smallest-growing, cream-flowered 'Tilford Cream'; and some relatively new like the orange-red 'Red Ace' and the pale pink 'Princess', whose flowers fade in prolonged, hot, dry weather (we should be so lucky!) to near-white.
Approx. height and spread after five years 80×80 cm ($2\frac{1}{2} \times 2\frac{1}{2}$ ft); after ten years 1×1 m (3×3 ft).

Stag's horn sumach (*Rhus typhina*) will also grow in sun as well as shade. (See page 82.)

Flowering currant (*Ribes sanguineum*) will grow in sun as well as shade. (See page 82.)

California tree poppy (*Romneya coulteri*) is a deciduous shrub which bears lovely, large, fragrant, white flowers with prominent gold centres, rather like poppies, from midsummer to mid-autumn. It dies back in winter and any shoots that don't die back should be pruned hard in spring.
Flowers Jul–Sept. Approx. height and spread after five years 1×1 m $(3 \times 3$ ft); after ten years 1×2 m $(3 \times 6$ ft).

Roses are essential for any garden, and they are now available in so many different forms that between them they'll do everything from climbing 20 m (60 ft) up a tree to growing in a window box! Though hybrid teas are the best-known roses and do produce superb blooms for cutting, their growth habit is rather stiff and ugly for mixed borders. Some of the cluster-flowered floribundas are more graceful, and of the many good ones – like the new, pale pink, superbly scented 'City of London', the blush-white 'Margaret Merril' and the amber-yellow 'Amber Queen' – are all excellent for a mixed border in a small garden. The new 'English' roses are also ideal for this purpose, combining the beautiful petal formations, soft colours and fragrance of the old roses, with a compact habit, repeat-flowering and disease resistance. There are many to choose from, but among those widely available are the soft yellow 'Graham Thomas', the white 'Fair Bianca' the peachy-pink 'Heritage', and 'Othello', with crimson flowers turning purple as they age.
Approx. height and spread after five years 80 cm–1.2 m $\times$ 80 cm–1.2 m $(2\frac{1}{2}$–4 ft $\times 2\frac{1}{2}$–4 ft).

For something even smaller, look for patio, dwarf or miniature roses – different places sell them under different names, though on the whole the two former are larger than the latter. Again there are many good ones from which to choose, and more are being addded all the time as the rose breeders realise there is a growing market for small roses. Among the best patio roses are the orange-red 'Anna Ford', the pale rose-pink 'Gentle Touch', the apricot-pink 'Peek a Boo', the golden-orange-flushed-with-pink 'Sweet Magic' (which sounds awful but looks stunning!), and the old favourite, 'The Fairy', with masses of clear pink rosettes from July to Christmas, given a mild autumn. Of the miniatures 'Baby Masquerade', with yellow flowers flushed pink, the three 'Sunblazes' ('Orange', 'Gold', and 'Pink'), the crimson 'Little Buckeroo' and the white 'Pour Toi' are all good.
Approx height and spread after five years 50–60 cm $\times$ 40–60 cm (18 in–2 ft $\times$ 16 in–2 ft).

Senecio greyii is grown largely for its soft, felty, silvery-green leaves, though it does produce bright acid-yellow, daisy-like flowers in midsummer. If you are growing it for its foliage and the flowers don't suit your colour scheme, simply cut off the buds when they appear.

Approx. height and spread after five years 60×80 cm ($2 \times 2\frac{1}{2}$ ft); after ten years 80 cm $\times 1.2$ m ($2\frac{1}{2} \times 4$ ft).

Spiraea has varieties which flower in spring, like *Spiraea × arguta* (also known as bridal wreath), and those that flower in summer. Some of these also have striking foliage, like *S. × bumalda* 'Gold-flame', whose new leaves emerge a startling orange-gold and slowly fade to green-gold by the time the dark pink-red flowers are coming through. Another rather curious variety worth thinking about is *S. japonica* 'Shirobana', which carries flowers that are all-white, all-rose-crimson or a mixture of the two at the same time.

Approx. height and spread after five years 40×50 cm (15×18 in); after ten years 60×70 cm (2×2 ft 3 in).

The low-growing, long-flowering dwarf rose 'The Fairy' is ideal for a mixed border in a small garden.

Lilacs (*Syringa* species) are beautiful, late spring- and early summer-flowering shrubs for a sunny spot on any soil, particularly a chalky

Above: A classic cottage garden border, with campanula, oriental poppies, delphiniums and hardy geraniums.

Left: Daisies (*Bellis perennis*) will also flower in light shade.

one. There are many excellent named varieties, though for small gardens you need to look for the pure white *Syringa* 'Vestale', the dark lilac-red *S.* 'Congo' or the pale yellow *S.* 'primrose'.
Approx. height and spread after five years 1 m × 90cm (3 × 2½ ft); after ten years 1.5 × 1.2 m (5 × 4 ft).

Alternatively, you could try the very slow-growing Korean lilac (*Syringa* meyeri 'Palibin' or 'Velutina'), which produces numerous sweetly scented, pinky-lilac flowers on a bush which reaches no more than 80 cm (2½ ft) in ten years. Slightly larger is *S. microphylla* 'Superba', which has rose-pink flowers in May and June and then again in the autumn. It's now possible to get lilacs which have been micro-propagated and so don't send up suckers from the rootstock.
Approx. height and spread after five years 30 × 25cm (12 × 10 in); after ten years 80 × 50 cm (2½ × 1½ ft).

Viburnum really is the most accommodating family of plants. As well as those that thrive in shade, there are many that need full sun. The winter-flowering varieties like *Viburnum × bodnantense* and *V. farreri*, which have sweetly scented, pink-white flowers on bare wood from November onwards, certainly need a sunny spot and will tolerate most soils, including limy ones. The winter-flowering evergreen, *V. tinus*, actually prefers a shadier position.
Approx. height and spread after five years 1.5 × 1m (5 × 3 ft); after ten years 2.5 × 2 m (8 × 6 ft).

The summer-flowering *Viburnum plicatum* 'Mariesii' has fresh green, deeply ribbed leaves and, in time, a distinctly layered habit, so the lace-caps of white flowers that appear on the tiered branches make them look as though they are covered in snow. It also has berries in autumn and good autumn colour. *V.p.* 'Watanabe' is a smaller version, reaching only two thirds the height and spread of 'Mariesii'. The guelder rose (*V. opulus*) will also grow in sun. (See page 66.)
Approx. height and spread after five years 2.5 × 2m (8 × 6 ft); after ten years 3.5 × 3 m (12 × 10 ft).

Weigela has pretty, white, pink or red, foxglove-like flowers in May and June. For flowers the ruby-red-flowered *Weigela* 'Bristol Ruby' and the bright scarlet *W.* 'Evita' are both good; while for the longest possible season of interest look for *W. florida* 'Foliis Purpureis', whose purple leaves tone perfectly with the paler purplish-pink flowers; and, perhaps best value of all, *W. florida* 'Variegata', which has pale pink flowers and very attractive cream and green variegated foliage through till the autumn.
Approx. height and spread after five years 1.2 × 1.2m (4 × 4 ft); after ten years 1.8 × 1.8 m (5½ × 5½ ft).

HERBACEOUS PLANTS

Bugle (*Ajuga reptans*), in its red and purple-leafed forms, is an excellent carpeter for a sunny border. Good varieties include *A. metallica*, which has dark purple, crinkly leaves; *A.r.* 'Braunherz', whose purple leaves have a bronze sheen; and *A.r.* 'Burgundy Glow', which has wine-red leaves. They all have spikes of deep blue flowers. Flowers Apr–Jun. Approx. height and spread 10 × 50 cm (4 × 18 in).

Pearly everlasting (*Anaphalis triplinervis* 'Summer Snow') carries pearly-white, everlasting daisies above clumps of grey foliage. Flowers Jul–Sept. Approx. height and spread 40 × 70 cm (16 in × 2 ft 3 in).

Anthemis cupaniana soon makes spreading mounds of fine-cut, silvery foliage, covered in early summer with chalk-white daisies. Flowers May–Jul. Approx. height and spread 30 × 40 cm (12 × 16 in).

Artemisia, in its many forms, is a superb silver foliage plant for a sunny border. One of the tallest and hardiest is *Artemisia absinthium* 'Lambrook Silver' with very fine, thread-like foliage and small, bobbly grey flowers, while *A. maritima* 'Powys Castle' is slightly smaller with the same fine silver foliage and no flowers. They keep their leaves all year, but look pretty scruffy by the spring, so prune hard to encourage fresh new growth. *A. ludoviciana* 'Silver Queen' has larger, deeply divided, silvery-white leaves. The smallest of all, *A. schmidtiana*, makes a low mound of silver thread-like foliage – good with a purple bugle or *Viola labradorica*. Flowers Jun–Jul. Approx. height and spread 10–90 cm × 30–60 cm (4 in–3 ft × 1–2 ft).

Michaelmas daisies (*Aster amellus*) are a must for autumn colour in a sunny border. The tall ones come in a range of colours – white and pink as well as the usual blue-mauve – and good varieties include *A.a.* 'King George', *A.a.* 'Violet Queen', and the pink *A.a.* 'Pink Zenith'. The dwarf Michaelmas daisies (*A. novi-belgii*) come in a similar range of colours plus red – *A.n.-b.* 'Jenny'. Good varieties include the soft lavender-mauve *A.n.-b.* 'Lady in Blue' and the warm coral pink *A.n.-b.* 'Alice Haslem'. Flowers Sept–Nov. Approx. height and spread 30–70 cm × 40–50 cm (1 ft–2 ft 3 in × 16–18 in).

Double daisy (*Bellis perennis*), with lots of pretty double flowers in early summer, is an old favourite, dating back to the sixteenth century and now enjoying a new wave of popularity. Good varieties include *B.p.* 'Dresden China', with shell-pink flowers; 'Alice' with peachy-pink flowers; and the 'hen and chicken' daisy, 'Prolifera', in which a ring of miniature daisies hangs from the central one. Flowers May–Jul. Approx. height and spread 10 × 15 cm (4 × 6 in).

Bellflowers (*Campanula* species), both the tall and the dwarf ones, are ideal plants for a sunny border. The very tall specimens like *Campanula lactiflora*, which can reach 1.5 m (5 ft) or more, have such large heads of powder-blue flowers that they really need staking if they are not to flop, so slightly smaller varieties like the blue or white *C. latifolia* or *C. persicifolia*, which produce stiff stems from neat rosettes of narrow evergreen leaves, are a better bet.

Flowers Jun–Aug. Approx. height and spread 90 × 40 cm (3 ft × 16 in).

The dwarf bellflowers, with upturned, cup-shaped or star-shaped flowers, are marvellous value for the front of a border as they go on flowering for months. Good varieties to look for include the blue *Campanula carpatica* 'Chewton Joy', 'Isobel' and 'Blue Moonlight', and 'Bressingham White'. 'Stella', which is smothered in small, star-shaped, blue flowers all summer, is another good variety. One to avoid is *C. porscharskyana*, which is a rampant spreader.

Flowers Jun–Sept. Approx. height and spread 20 × 40 cm (8 × 16 in).

Weigela praecox 'Variegata' is attractive in flower but worth growing for its foliage alone.

Mountain cornflower (*Centaurea montana*), a relative of the more widely grown annual, has lovely, scented, deep blue flowers above mats of green-grey foliage. If you cut it back after flowering, it will bloom again in autumn.

Flowers Jul–Aug. Approx. height and spread 50 × 50 cm (18 × 18 in).

Red hot pokers
(*Kniphofia galpinii*) and
Sedum 'Autumn Joy'
provide an arresting
contrast in flower colour,
foliage shape and form.

Shasta daisies (*Chrysanthemum maximum*) are invaluable white flowers for any border, flowering from midsummer to autumn. Good varieties include the tall 'Wirral Supreme' and the much smaller 'Snowcap', which is little more than half its size. Other border chrysanthemums (as opposed to their much larger-headed, show-bench relatives) for colour in late summer include the orange *C. rubellum* 'Peterkin', the rich mahogany red *C.r.* 'Duchess of Edinburgh' and the pale apricot-yellow, *C.r.* 'Mary Stoker'.
Flowers Jul–Nov. Approx. height and spread 60 cm–1 m × 30–40 cm (2–3 ft × 12–16 in).

Crocosmia, which used to be called montbretia, adds a blaze of colour from late June onwards, with its fiery orange flowers. Good hybrids include the flame-red *Crocosmia × crocosmiiflora* 'Lucifer', the deep, burnt orange 'Emberglow' and, for something altogether softer, the pale apricot yellow 'Solfatare'.
Flowers Jul–Sept. Approx. height and spread 70 × 40 cm (2 ft 3 in × 16 in).

Delphiniums are without doubt the most spectacular blue-flowered cottage garden plants, and now there are dwarf varieties available they're suitable for the smallest garden. The varieties to look for are Belladona hybrids like D. × *belladonna* 'Lamartine', 'Peace' and

'Blue Bees', and even smaller dwarf hybrids like *D. elatum* 'Blue Fountains' and 'Blue Heaven'. The only problems with growing delphiniums is that if the soil is too wet and heavy they will rot, and that the slugs like the young leaves almost as much as hosta leaves, so take precautions. (If you don't want to use pellets, 10 cm (4 in) rings cut from plastic lemonade bottles and pushed into the soil around the young plants work pretty well.)
Flowers Jun–Aug. Approx. height and spread 80 cm–1.2 m × 50–80 cm ($2\frac{1}{2}$–4 ft × $1\frac{1}{2}$–$2\frac{1}{2}$ ft).

Cone flower (*Echinacea purpurea*) is another good late summer-flowering plant for a sunny border. Its rich mauve-red petals slope away from the large central cone which is a golden brown. Good varieties include 'Robert Bloom'.
Flowers Jul–Sept. Approx. height and spread 90 × 40 cm (3 ft × 16 in).

Spurges (*Euphorbia* species) do well in practically every garden situation, and of those that like a sunny spot and moist soil, two forms of *E. griffithii* are outstanding. 'Fireglow' has fiery-red flower heads above attractive light green foliage, while 'Dixter' has deeper orange-red flowers and leaves and stems tinged with a chestnut red.
Flowers Jun–Aug. Approx. height and spread 75 × 40 cm ($2\frac{1}{2}$ ft × 16 in).

Cranesbills (*Geranium* species) are another large family with members in all shapes and sizes, the flowers ranging from white through blues, pinks and almost fluorescent magenta to a purple so deep it's almost black. Among the most widely available varieties are *G. endressii* 'Wargrave Pink', which produces its salmon-pink flowers from May to November, and 'Johnson's Blue', which has clear blue, cup-shaped flowers for many weeks in midsummer. Not so widely available but worth seeking out are *G. renardii*, which has lovely, scalloped, sage-green leaves and blush-white flowers veined with purple; *G. sanguineum*, with a profusion of vivid magenta flowers all summer; and the trailing *G. wallichianum* 'Buxton's Blue', which produces trailing stems of blue flowers with a white eye from midsummer to autumn. (It's an ideal plant for growing among small, early summer-flowering plants, because once their flowers have finished, it can trail over them, putting its own flowers in their place.
Flowers May–Nov. Approx. height and spread 40 × 40 cm (16 × 16 in).

Avens (*Geum* species) is an easy-to-grow plant, forming slowly spreading clumps of rich green leaves and producing brightly col-oured flowers in shades of yellow and red. Good varieties include the yellow *Geum coccineum* 'Lady Stratheden' and the brick-red *G.c.* 'Mrs Bradshaw'.
Flowers May–Aug. Approx. height and spread 50 × 40 cm (18 × 16 in).

Baby's breath (*Gypsophila* species) produces sprays of tiny white flowers. Its botanical name means 'chalk lover', so it will obviously thrive on limy soil and dislikes acid conditions. The best white form is *Gypsophila paniculata* 'Bristol White' and there's a very pretty pink one called 'Rosy Veil'. The dwarf varieties, such as *G. repens* 'Dorothy Teacher', like even drier conditions.
Flowers Jun–Sept. Approx. height and spread 90 × 70 cm (3 ft × 2 ft 3 in).

Day lilies (*Hemerocallis* species) bear flowers that last for only a day, but they are produced in such profusion over many weeks that it doesn't matter. They also form weed-smothering clumps of bright green, strap-like leaves. There are many, many different ones – indeed, there is even a Hemerocallis Society – but a few good varieties that are fairly easily available include the velvety, bright yellow *Hemerocallis* 'Canary Glow', the old, sweetly scented, pale primrose 'Whichford', and the warm peachy-pink 'Pink Damask'.
Flowers Jun–Sept. Approx. height and spread 75 × 50 cm ($2\frac{1}{2} \times 1\frac{1}{2}$ ft).

Heuchera sanguinea (Coral flower) will grow in sun as well as shade. (See page 71.)

Houttuynia cordata **'Chamaeleon'** has superb, red, cream and green variegated foliage which quickly spreads to form a bright mat. It does have white flowers, but they're insignificant.
Approx. height and spread 20 × 70 cm (8 in × 2 ft 3 in).

Iris (*Iris kaempferi* and *I. sibirica*) will thrive in a sunny spot provided the soil is always moist. *I.k.* 'Variegata' has lovely cream and green striped leaves with pale mauve flowers, while the smaller *I.k.* 'Alba' bears beautiful white flowers. Good varieties of *I. sibirica* include 'Alba', 'Flight of Butterflies', with rich blue flowers veined in white, and 'Papillon', with flowers of the softest blue.
Flowers Jun–Aug. Approx. height and spread 60–90 cm × 30 cm (2–3 ft × 1 ft).

Red hot pokers (*Kniphofia* species), as their name suggests, usually have flowers in glowing orange or red, though there are some forms now available with ivory flowers, green in bud (*Kniphofia* 'Little Maid'), and cream flowers, red in bud ('Strawberries and Cream'). If you plant them in autumn, they should be protected with a heap of bracken or straw for the first winter.
Flowers Jul–Oct. Approx. height and spread 60 cm–1.2 m × 70 cm (2–4 ft × 2 ft 3 in).

Ligularias combine handsome foliage with attractive flowers, though different forms have very different flowers. *Ligularia dentata* bears large, yellow or orange, daisy-like flowers, while *L. steno-*

cephala 'The Rocket' has tall spikes of small, yellow flowers, not unlike those of bugbane, on black stems. Don't worry if they wilt in hot weather – they'll soon recover, though they should never go short of water.

Flowers Jul–Sept. Approx. height and spread 1.5 m × 70 cm (5 ft × 2 ft 3 in).

Peonies (*Paeonia* species) undoubtedly have the most beautiful flowers in spring, but in the majority of cases their flowering season is too short, the space they occupy too large and their foliage too dull to make them good plants for small gardens. The exception is *Paeonia mlokosewitschii* – known to its many friends, for understandable reasons, as 'mlok' or 'Molly the witch' – which is attractive from the time its crimson shoots start pushing their way through the soil in winter. They are followed by buds and leaves, at first tinged pinkish bronze, then becoming a soft grey-green, and the most beautiful large, pale lemon flowers with gold centres. In autumn its unusual seed pods split open to reveal rows of red and blue-black seeds.

Flowers Apr–May. Approx. height and spread 60 × 60 cm (2 × 2 ft).

Oriental poppies (*Papaver orientalis*) are traditional cottage garden plants with their big, blowsy flower heads, not only in the traditional orange-scarlet, but also in different shades of pink, like *P.o.* 'Mrs Perry'; mauve, like 'Blue Moon'; and even black and white! They are inclined to flop, and the foliage may start to die off in midsummer, so be sure to plant them next to or behind something that flowers later.

Flowers May–Jun. Approx. height and spread 80 × 50 cm ($2\frac{1}{2}$ × $1\frac{1}{2}$ ft).

Phlox (*Phlox paniculata*) are also something no self-respecting cottage garden would be without, for their long-lasting, bright flowers range across many shades from white through various pinks and mauves to scarlet and crimson. Good, widely available varieties include *P.p.* 'Balmoral', 'Border Gem', 'Prince of Orange' and 'White Admiral'.

Flowers Jul–Sept. Approx. height and spread 90 × 50 cm (3 × $1\frac{1}{2}$ ft).

The dwarf phlox, *P. douglasii* and *P. subulata*, form low mats of green foliage and produce masses of flowers in the same range of colours as their larger relation, plus blue. Good ones to look for include *P.d.* 'Red Admiral' and 'May Snow', *P.s.* 'Oakington Blue', 'Temiscaming' (a vivid rosy red) and 'White Delight'.

Flowers May–Jul. Approx. height and spread 15 × 40 cm (6 × 16 in).

Jacob's ladder (*Polemonium caeruleum*), yet another old cottage garden favourite, gets its name from its ladder-like, bright green foliage, and has clusters of mid-blue flowers throughout the

Above: Traditional cottage garden plants like oriental poppies and campanulas are ideal for sunny, south-facing borders.

Left: Ornamental grasses, like the moisture-loving golden sedge (*Carex stricta* 'Bowles' Golden'), are valuable foliage plants.

summer. Once it's established, it seeds itself freely, but is easily hoed out if it becomes a nuisance.

Flowers May–Aug. Approx. height and spread 70 × 50 cm (2 ft 3 in × 18 in).

Ornamental rhubarb (*Rheum* species) is a dramatic foliage plant, though in most of its forms it's too large for a small garden. The exception is *Rheum* 'Ace of Hearts', which has dark green, heart-shaped leaves, veined and backed with crimson, and plumes of dainty, very pale pink flowers.

Flowers May–Jun. Approx. height and spread 1.2 × 1 m (4 × 3 ft).

Rudbeckia brings a warm glow to the late summer/early autumn border, with golden yellow or orange daisy flowers with their

prominent dark central cones. Look for *Rudbeckia fulgida* (or *newmanii*) 'Deamii' or 'Goldsturm'.
Flowers Jul–Oct. Approx. height and spread 80–40 cm ($2\frac{1}{2}$ ft × 16 in).

Scabious (*Scabiosa caucasia* 'Clive Greaves'), which likes limy soil, produces large, violet-blue flowers from midsummer on. *S.c.* 'Floral Queen' has bigger blue flowers, while there is a creamy-white form, 'Miss Wilmott'.
Flowers Jun–Sept. Approx. height and spread 70 × 50 cm (2 ft 3 in × 18 in).

Kaffir lily (*Schizostylis coccinea* 'Major') produces neat, grass-like foliage and cherry-red flowers in late autumn at a time when there is little else so vivid in flower. It needs some protection in winter: bracken or straw piled over the leaves once flowering is finished.
Flowers Oct–Nov. Approx. height and spread 75 × 40 cm ($2\frac{1}{2}$ ft × 16 in.)

Tradescantia virginiana, yet another lovely plant discovered by the Tradescants, the seventeenth-century plant hunters, has lovely three-petalled flowers in different shades of blue. The most vivid is *T.v.* 'Isis', with bright gold stamens, and there's a fine white form, 'Innocence'.
Flowers Jun–Sept. Approx. height and spread 40 × 40 cm (16 × 16 in).

Ornamental grasses
There are also some ornamental grasses that deserve a place in a sunny mixed border.

***Holcus mollis* 'Variegatus'** has variegated green and white leaves, with the white predominating, especially when the new growth appears in spring and again in autumn. It will also grow in partial shade, and though it can be invasive, it's easily pulled out.
Approx. height 15 cm (6 in).

Miscanthus sinensis is a dramatic plant for the back of a border, making clumps up to 2 m (6 ft) tall. The tallest is *M.s.* 'Silver Feather', with narrow, green leaves and plumes of silvery-pink in autumn. Slightly smaller, *M.s.* 'Variegatus' has strongly variegated green and white leaves arching from rigid stems, while the unusual *M.s.* 'Zebrinus' has dark green leaves marked with distinct, horizontal, yellow bands.
Approx. height 1.5–2 m (5–6 ft).

***Molinia caerulea* 'Variegata'** has short, neat tufts of green and cream leaves, with arching stems of tiny, feathery flowers in late summer, both of which fade to an attractive pale beige in winter.
Approx. height 50 cm (18 in).

ANNUALS

When it comes to choosing annuals for a sunny border with reasonably moisture-retentive soil, the world is your oyster, for they'll flower here better than anywhere else. Annuals fall into two groups – half-hardies, which need to be sown indoors and planted out only after all danger of frost has gone, and hardies, which can be sown straight into the soil. We're assuming that, this year, you won't have time or space to grow your half-hardies from seed, so you'll be buying them from the garden centre towards the end of May or even in early June. You'll see half-hardy bedding plants on sale from as early as late March, but don't buy unless you have a greenhouse in which to protect them until the weather warms up.

How you plant your annuals – whether in neat, straight lines, dotted here and there, or in bold drifts – is, as always, a matter of taste. There are no prizes for guessing which we prefer!

Some good half-hardy annuals to buy as plants

Flowering from July to October

Ageratum makes low mounds of fluffy, blue flowers throughout the summer. *Ageratum houstonianum* 'Blue Mink' is perhaps the most widely available variety, but newer hybrids, like *A.h.* 'Blue Danube' and 'North Sea', form bushier, even more free-flowering plants. Approx. height 15–30 cm (4–10 in).

Asters are good, late summer-flowering plants in many different shades of white, yellow, pink, salmon, carmine, mauve and blue. The taller varieties provide cut flowers too, while the dwarf varieties are good for the front of the border. Approx. height 20–75 cm (8 in–$2\frac{1}{2}$ ft).

Begonias (*Begonia semperflorens*), the fibrous-rooted kind, are not to everyone's taste, but they are unbeatable for providing bright colour – vivid reds, pinks, salmons, white – at the front of a border right through the summer, regardless of how dreadful the weather. (See page 74.) Approx. height 15–30 cm (6–12 in).

Cosmos (*Cosmea* species), which produces lovely, open, daisy-like flowers in shades of red, pink and white above very feathery, bright green foliage, is an excellent annual for the middle of the border. Approx. height 90 cm (3 ft).

Busy lizzie (*Impatiens* species) will flower in sun as well as shade. (See page 74.)

Lobelia. (See page 74.)

Marigolds, the French and African kinds, seem to divide the world into those who love them and those who hate them! But they are very easy to grow, will put up with dreadful weather and flower right through the summer. They range from giant drumsticks, like 'Doubloon', which are 90 cm (3 ft) tall with flowers 13 cm (5 in) across, to dwarf French marigolds, like the gold-edged 'Red Marietta', only 20 cm (8 in) high. Although *Tagetes* is the botanical name for African and French marigolds, only the very dwarf ones, *T. pumila*, are sold under that name. *T.p.* 'Lemon Gem', 'Tangerine Gem' and 'Golden Gem' are all good.
Approx. height 20–90 cm (8 in–3 ft).

Nemesias come in practically every colour of the rainbow. You can buy them only in mixed colours.
Approx. height 25 cm (10 in).

Tobacco plants (*Nicotiana* species) also come in a wide range of colours – everything from wine red to lime green. The smaller hybrids, like *Nicotiana alata* 'Domino' or 'Roulette', stand up to the rigours of a typical English summer better than the taller varieties and present their flowers upwards rather than drooping down. For the best perfume it's worth tracking down *N. affinis*. It's tall – 75 cm ($2\frac{1}{2}$ ft) – and its white flowers aren't large, but the smell on a warm summer evening is reason enough to grow it.
Approx. height 30 cm (1 ft).

Petunias really are a monument to the plant breeders' art, for they now come not only in every colour you can imagine, but also with white edging, with stripes, with stars, double as well as single, frilled as well as plain. The choice is yours, though heavy rain can still make a mess of many of them. Resisto hybrids are bred specially to stand up to the weather.
Approx. height 25–30 cm (9–12 in).

Verbena is sometimes available in single colours, but more usually as a mixture. *Verbena × hybrida* 'Showtime' is particularly good, making an effective weed-suppressing carpet.
Approx. height 25–30 cm (10–12 in).

A few good hardy annuals

Alyssum is the traditional edging companion for lobelia – they are sold together in street markets as 'blue and white'! It's also good for rock gardens, and in between paving slabs. Once you've sown it, you've always got it, for it seeds itself freely every year. The largest-flowered variety yet is *Alyssum maritimum* 'Snow Crystals', though *A.m.* 'Carpet of Snow' is also a good one.
Approx. height 10 cm (4 in).

Naturalised winter-flowering bulbs – *Crocus tomasinianus*, snowdrops (*Galanthus nivalis*) and winter aconites (*Eranthis hyemalis*).

Pot marigolds, or English marigolds, are lovely old cottage garden annuals in a range of colours from creamy yellow to burnt orange. Good varieties include *Calendula officinalis* 'Pacific Beauty' and the much smaller *C.o.* 'Fiesta Gitana'.
Approx. height 30–60 cm (1–2 ft).

Candytuft (*Iberis* species) has clusters of small flowers in shades of pink, lavender, carmine and white. It's easy to grow and long-flowering. *Iberis umbellata* 'Fairy Mixture' (or 'Mixed') is a good variety.
Approx. height 25 cm (10 in).

Clarkia is an upright annual that produces double flowers in shades of red, pink and white that could pass for carnations at a distance. *Clarkia elegans* 'Choice Double Mixed' is among the best.
Approx. height 50 cm (18 in).

Cornflowers (*Centaurea* species) now come in a range of colours, but, to the traditionalists among us, they still look best in deep, rich blue. A good tall variety is *Centaurea cyanus* 'Blue Diadem', while 'Baby Blue' has similar flowers but grows to less than half the size.
Approx. height 30–75 cm (1–2½ ft).

Godetias have lovely, delicate-looking flowers like upturned bells, in shades of pink, salmon red and white, with many bi-colours among them. *Godetia grandiflora* 'Sybil Sherwood', a rich salmon pink edged in white, is one of the most beautiful.
Approx. height 30 cm (1 ft).

Mallow (*Lavatera trimensis*) is a stunning, easy-to-grow plant for the middle of a border, producing large trumpets of pink or gleaming white flowers for months on end. *L.t.* 'Silver Cup', a rich silver-pink, and *L.t.* 'Mont Blanc', a pure white, are both established favourites, while a new, paler mauve-pink variety, *L.t.* 'Pink Beauty', seems set to join them.
Approx. height 60 cm (2 ft).

Poached egg flower (*Limnanthes douglasii*) is perfectly named, for its small, egg-yolk-yellow flowers are rimmed with white. It's a low-growing annual, ideal for the front of the border, especially with other yellow and white flowering plants.
Approx. height 15 cm (6 in).

Mignonette (*Reseda odorata*) has curious, tiny flowers of yellowish-green and red which give off a superb fragrance, both night and morning. Bees love it.
Approx. height 30 cm (1 ft).

Love-in-a-mist (*Nigella damascena*) is yet another cottage garden plant, with cornflower-blue blooms surrounded by a mist of fine, green foliage. 'Miss Jekyll' is the best blue, while for the more radical among us the mixed pinks, blues and whites of 'Persian Jewels' are worth trying.
Approx. height 60 cm (2 ft).

Sunflowers (*Helianthus annuus*), certainly the giant kind, 'Giant Yellow' or 'Tall Single', are great fun for children – and parrot owners, since the enormous centres produce masses of seeds, which

wild birds also like. Not as tall, and with smaller, chrysanthemum-like, double flowers, the variety 'Sungold Double' is good for the back of a border.
Approx. height 1.2–1.8 m + (4–6 ft +).

Climbing annuals

Canary creeper (*Tropaeolum peregrinum*) is a lovely climber for a sunny fence or for growing through a shrub. It has fresh green leaves and fluffy bright yellow flowers that remind you rather of Woodstock in the Snoopy cartoon.
Approx. height 3 m (10 ft).

Sweet peas (*Lathyrus odoratus*) can be treated like other annuals and sown straight into the ground, but the best results come from seed sown under glass in autumn or early spring. Starting them on windowsills isn't very satisfactory as they tend to become very leggy, not bushy as they should be, so if you haven't got a greenhouse or cold frame, you're better off buying them as young plants from the garden centre. There are dozens of different colours to choose from, but try to buy a sweetly scented variety.
Approx. height 2 m (6 ft).

BULBS

In a sunny spot and a moisture-retentive but not heavy soil you can grow practically any bulbs you like, summer- and autumn-flowering, as well as spring-flowering, so you can afford to be choosy.

Ornamental onions (*Allium* species) are dramatic bulbs for sunny borders. They range from the small *A. moly*, which has clusters of butter-yellow flowers in June, to the striking *A. christophii* (*albopilosum*), with heads of silvery-lilac flowers the size of grapefruit on stems 60 cm (2 ft) high. Also good and easy to find is the small, rosy-pink-flowered *A. ostrowskianum*.
Flowers May–Jul. Approx height 6–60 cm (10 in–2 ft). Plant 10–20 cm (4–8 in) apart depending on the size of the bulb.

Anemones, particularly *Anemone blanda* and *A. nemorosa*, our native wood anemone, are excellent for a sunny border, though the latter would be happier in dappled shade from some shrubs. *A. blanda* has large, daisy-like flowers in white, pink or blue and, given decent soil, will soon multiply into a large patch. The wood anemone has smaller flowers, white flushed with a mauve-pink on the outside, and finely cut leaves.
Flowers Mar–May. Approx. height 10 cm (4 in). Plant 10 cm (4 in) apart.

Glory of the snow (*Chionodoxa luciliae*) likes sun as well as shade. (See page 75.)

Crocuses are a must for any sunny border, and there's a huge choice. There are large-flowered Dutch crocuses (*Crocus vernus*) in shades of gold ('Yellow Mammoth'), white ('Jeanne d'Arc'), purple ('Paulus Potter'), purple-and-white ('Pickwick'), and the smaller species crocuses (*C. chrysanthus*), often in softer colours: look out for 'Blue Pearl', a delicate pale blue with a pearly sheen, 'Cream Beauty' and 'Snow Bunting', pure white with a gold centre.
Flowers Feb–Apr. Approx. height 5–12 cm (2–5 in). Plant 8 cm (3 in) apart.

Snowdrops (*Galanthus nivalis*) will thrive in sun as well as shade. (See page 77.)

Summer hyacinth (*Galtonia candicans*) is an undervalued summer-flowering bulb with tall spires of sweetly scented, waxy-white flowers. The leaves are long and rather floppy, so these bulbs are best planted among shrubs or herbaceous plants which can disguise them.
Flowers Jul–Aug. Approx. height 90 cm (3 ft). Plant 15 cm (6 in) apart.

Hyacinths do have the most marvellous scent and, with their fat, densely packed heads of flowers, are an ideal way of creating large splashes of colour in a sunny border. Good varieties include the deep blue *Hyacinthus orientalis* 'Ostara', the pure white 'L'In-nocence', the rich pink 'Jan Bos' and the pale yellow 'City of Haarlem'. Make sure that you don't buy the bulbs prepared for forcing indoors since they aren't suitable for planting outside. Hya-cinths are best treated as bedding plants and lifted after flowering.
Flowers Apr–May. Approx. height 25 cm (10 in). Plant 15 cm (6 in) apart.

Dwarf irises (*Iris reticulata*) are stunning miniatures in many shades of blue, from the pale blue 'Cantab' to the deep reddish purple 'J. S. Dijt', all with delicate 'iris' markings on the lower petals. *I. danfordiae* is a vivid yellow iris of the same size; often, after flowering, it breaks up into smaller, non-flowering bulblets, so for all practical purposes you have lost it. Deeper planting – 12 cm (5 in) instead of 8 cm (3 in) – helps to prevent this happening.
Flowers Feb–Mar. Approx. height 15 cm (6 in). Plant 10 cm (4 in) apart.

Lilies are so exotic-looking and have such a wonderful fragrance that you might assume they are difficult to grow. Certainly some are difficult, but others are very easy, given a soil that isn't wet enough in winter to rot them and that doesn't dry out in summer. They're tall-growing, but if you plant them among shrubs or per-ennials, they will support them and they won't need staking. Try *Lilium regale*, which has large, white trumpets, flushed pink on the outside, with such a heady perfume that a potful on a patio can scent a whole house through an open window. They prefer having

their roots in shade and their heads in the sun, so planting them among small shrubs is an ideal way of growing them. *L. henryi*, which has large, hanging, orange 'Turk's-cap' flowers in late summer, is also easy, and some of the Asiatic hybrids, like the orange-red *L*. 'Enchantment' and the white *L*. 'Sterling Star', speckled with brown, are all worth a try. These lilies are lime-tolerant and are all stem-rooting, so should be planted quite deeply – about 20 cm (8 in).
Flowers Jun–Sept. Approx. height 1–2 m (3–6 ft). Plant 20 cm (8 in) apart.

Grape hyacinths (*Muscari* species) grow in sun as well as shade. (See page 77.)

Daffodils (*Narcissus* species) really do herald the arrival of spring, and no garden, no matter how small, should be without them. In a small garden some of the more common, large daffodils, like 'King Alfred', take up a lot of space and look rather out of proportion. Dwarf ones are a better bet, and apart from *Narcissus cyclamineus* 'February Gold' and *N.c.* 'Tête à Tête' (see page 78) that also tolerate shade, there are many to choose from that thrive in full sun. Look for hybrids of *N.c.*, like 'Jack Snipe' and the white and pale primrose 'Dove Wings', and the jonquil narcissi like the deep lemon *N. jonquilla* 'Sundial' and the popular yellow and orange *N.j.* 'Suzy'. In a very small space try angel's tears (*N. triandrus alba*) which has two or three small, creamy white flowers on 15 cm (6 in) stems or, from the same family, the slightly taller, free-flowering, robust, butter-yellow 'Hawera' or the exquisite pure-white-flowered 'Thalia'.
Flowers Feb–Apr. Approx. height 15–30 cm (6–12 in). Plant 8 cm (3 in) apart.

Nerine (*Nerine bowdenii*) is a valuable, autumn-flowering bulb for a sunny, sheltered spot (the foot of a south-facing wall is ideal). It bears a head of bright pink flowers with curly petals on a slender stem. The strap-like leaves follow the flowers, but die down in early summer. The bulbs should be planted with the neck level with the surface of the soil.
Flowers Sept–Nov. Approx. height 50 cm (18 in). Plant 10–15 cm (4–6 in) apart.

Star of Bethlehem (*Ornithogalum umbellatum*) has heads of starry white flowers, which are green on the outside, in late spring. Unlike its relative, *O. nutans* (see page 87), it needs full sun.
Flowers Apr–May. Approx. height 23 cm (9 in). Plant 8 cm (3 in) apart.

Tulips are another must for the late spring garden, though again some of the smaller species tulips are probably the best bet. For one thing they are smaller, more in scale with small gardens and less likely to get flattened by hurricane-force April showers; and for another, many of the tall garden tulips really need lifting and storing once they've finished flowering – something that few first time gardeners have the facilities to do. Look for Kaufmanniana, Gregii or Fosteriana hybrids which flower early and in many cases have attractive variegated leaves as well as lovely flowers. Of the Kaufmannianas, 'Heart's Delight', blush-white with carmine outside, 'Showwinner', a glowing cardinal red, and the creamy white 'Concerto' are all outstanding. Of the Greigiis, look for the deep rose 'Oratorio', the salmon-orange 'Toronto', with two or three flowers on each stem, and the vivid red 'Red Riding Hood'. Among the best Fosterianas, which have slightly longer flowers, are the three 'Emperors' – 'Red', 'Orange' and 'Yellow'. Also lovely are *Tulipa tarda*, whose butter-yellow flowers with a white edging open almost flat; the lovely, rounded, apricot-yellow *T. batalinii* 'Bright Gem'; and a true miniature, *T. linofolia*, with brilliant scarlet flowers on stems 10–12 cm (4–5 in) high.

Flowers Mar–May. Approx. height 15–25 cm (6–10 in). Plant 10 cm (4 in) apart.

Dry Soil

If you have a dry, sunny border, the sort of plants you are looking for are those whose native habitat is the thin, dry soil of the Mediterranean area. And if the picture that conjures up in your mind is of the tough, straggly, dusty specimens you've seen growing on the roadside in Spain, a look at Beth Chatto's Mediterranean or Dry Garden in Essex will show you just how beautiful such plants can be. Beth's gravelly soil in that part of the garden was so thin and dry, she says, when she first took over the garden, that even native British weeds used to shrivel up and die!

Almost all grey- and silver-leafed plants – lavender, artemisias, lamb's ears (*Stachys lanata*) and rock roses (*Cistus* species) – will thrive in these conditions, for what gives the leaves their silvery colour is a covering of very fine hairs which acts like a sunscreen to prevent the leaf scorching or shrivelling up. Other 'fleshy' plants, like stonecrops (*Sedum* species) or houseleeks (*Sempervivum* species), protect themselves against drought by being able to store water in their leaves, while still others, such as the sun-loving spurges (*Euphorbia* species) have a waxy coating to protect their surface. Few drought lovers have large leaves – they have either very small ones, like the cotton lavender (*Santolina chamaecyparis*), or very thin ones, like pinks (*Dianthus* species), or very finely divided ones, like the artemisias, so they don't lose moisture that way. Bergenias are an exception here, but then their leaves are as tough as leather anyway and so in no danger of shrivelling up.

A number of these Mediterranean plants – rosemary, lemon verbena (*Lippia citriodora*) and lavender – also have aromatic oils in their leaves which helps protect them, and which is released into the air when the leaves are crushed or even just brushed against. That makes them good plants for the front of a border or on the corner of a busy thoroughfare, where that is most likely to happen.

In Beth Chatto's Dry Garden flower colours are important – stunning 'hot' shades like the vivid magenta pink of rose campion (*Lychnis coronaria*), the vivid blue of the globe thistle (*Echinops ritro*) and the intense scarlet of *Anemone fulgens*. But as most drought-loving plants produce rather small flowers, they usually appear, as she puts it, as small, vivid dots of colour against a largely, though not exclusively, grey background.

Since foliage plays such an important part in maintaining a long season of interest in a dry garden, it's vital to include plenty of contrasts, not just in the colours – golds and deep green like that of the perennial candytuft (*Iberis saxatilis*) as well as blues and greys – but in the shapes of the plants themselves, as well as in the shapes of the leaves. You want round shapes and spiky ones, horizontals and verticals. In Beth's view, mound-forming plants like lavender, cotton lavender, ballota and rue will look like 'buns in a baking tray' unless you have some tall, spiky plants or ornamental grasses planted among them. Even at the front of a border, where you will naturally place smaller plants, something upright, like the steely-blue grass *Festuca glauca* makes all the difference.

CLIMBERS
Climbing hydrangea (*Hydrangea petiolaris*). (See page 58.)

Passionflower (*Passiflora caerulea*). (See page 138.)

SHRUBS
Barberry (*Berberis thunbergii*), in its pink, red and purple forms. (See page 139.)

Buddleia. (See page 139.)

Blue spiraea (*Caryopteris incana* × *mongolica* 'Arthur Simmonds', still sometimes sold as C. × *clandonensis*) is a low-growing shrub with green-grey foliage and clusters of pale violet-blue flowers in late summer–early autumn. All its shoots should be cut back to near ground level in mid-spring, and for that reason it never grows larger than 80×80 cm ($2\frac{1}{2} \times 2\frac{1}{2}$ ft). Good varieties to look out for are C.*i*. 'Heavenly Blue', with bright blue flowers, and C.*i*. 'Kew Blue', with darker blue flowers.
Flowers Jul–Oct. Approx. height and spread in one season 80×80 cm ($2\frac{1}{2} \times 2\frac{1}{2}$ ft).

Beth Chatto's Dry
Garden in spring (above)
and again in midsummer.

Wintersweet (*Chimonanthus praecox*). (See page 115.)

Rock roses (*Cistus* species) produce a succession of single, flat flowers in a range of colours from white, both pure and attractively blotched with crimson or purple, through various shades of pink to crimson. The flowers last only a day but they are born in such profusion that it doesn't matter. Many rock roses have attractive grey foliage, but only a few varieties are reliably hardy. Look out for the small *Cistus × corbariensis*, with small, white flowers opening from buds tinted crimson; C. 'Silver Pink', with (not surprisingly) silver-pink flowers borne in clusters; the tall *C. × cyprius*, with large, white flowers blotched with crimson; and the equally tall *C. laurifolius*, which has leathery, dark blue-green leaves and white flowers with yellow centres. They like any dry soil, including lime.
Flowers Jun–Jul. Approx. height and spread after five years 60 cm–1.2 m × 60 cm–1.2 m (2–4 ft × 2–4 ft); after ten years 80 cm–2 m × 80 cm–2 m ($2\frac{1}{2}$–6 ft × $2\frac{1}{2}$–6 ft).

Coronilla glauca is a rounded, bushy evergreen with lovely foliage not unlike that of wisteria only blue-green in colour. It produces masses of golden-yellow pea flowers in early summer and then intermittently throughout the summer and autumn. It can be fan-trained against a sunny wall.
Flowers May/Jun–Sept. Approx. height and spread after five years 1.5 × 1.5m (5 × 5 ft); after ten years 2 × 2 m (6 × 6 ft).

Smoke bush (*Cotinus cogyggria*) in its red-leafed forms, like 'Notcutt's Variety', will tolerate dry conditions. (See page 141.)

Moroccan broom (*Cytisus battandieri*) will do well on a sunny wall. (See page 136.)

Broom (*Cytisus* species). (See page 142.)

Spindle (*Euonymus fortunei*) will tolerate dry soil once established. Water in times of drought during its first year. (See page 79.)

***Fremontodendron californicum*.** (See page 143.)

Mount etna broom (*Genista aetnensis*) makes a very large, graceful, arching shrub whose branches are smothered in bright yellow pea flowers, making a golden fountain in summer. It does eventually grow into a very large shrub, and doesn't respond well to pruning once it's mature, so allow plenty of space for it.
Flowers Jul–Aug. Approx. height and spread after five years 2.5 × 2.5m (8 × 8 ft); after ten years 3.5 × 3.5 m (12 × 12 ft).

Spanish gorse (*Genista hispanica*), which has lighter yellow flowers, makes a much smaller bush (60 cm × 1 m (2 × 3 ft) after ten years), very prickly and rounded, while G. *lydia*, which in the same time reaches only 60 cm (2 ft) in height but achieves a spread of 2 m (6 ft), is ideal for a dry bank or for tumbling over a wall.

Hypericum patulum 'Hidcote'. (See page 143.)

Lavender is an ideal shrub for a dry, sunny situation, with its narrow, silvery foliage and spikes of strongly scented lavender-blue flowers all summer long. It can be planted and clipped to make a low, informal hedge or edging to a border, or allowed to grow into a rounded bush. Good varieties include *Lavandula spica*, the old English lavender; the dark lavender-blue dwarf *Lavandula angustifolia* 'Munstead'; and the even smaller 'Hidcote', with the most silvery foliage and the most intense blue flowers. You can also plant white- or pink-flowered lavenders – L.*a.* 'Alba' or the dwarf L.*a.* 'Nana Alba' or 'Lodden Pink'.
Flowers Jul–Sept. Approx. height and spread after five years 20–50 cm × 40–60 cm (8–18 in × 16 in–2 ft); after ten years 30–80 cm × 30–80 cm (1–2$\frac{1}{2}$ ft × 1–2$\frac{1}{2}$ ft).

Russian sage (*Perovskia atriplicifolia*) loves dry, sunny conditions and, if it gets them, grows into a tall spire of very thin stems so silvery they are almost white. These are covered in spikes of lavender-blue flowers in late summer. The best form is one called 'Blue Spire'. It should be cut back hard each spring to encourage really silvery new stems and to prevent it outgrowing the space allowed for it.
Flowers Aug–Sept. Approx. height and spread in one season 90 × 60 cm (3 × 2 ft).

Jerusalem sage (*Phlomis fruticosa*) is another grey-leaved shrub from the Mediterranean, with long, slightly wavy leaves that look rather like a giant version of sage leaves and clusters of pale yellow flowers in summer. The young foliage is the most attractive, so it needs to be pruned back in spring.
Flowers Jun–Jul. Approx. height and spread after five years 1 × 1m (3 × 3 ft); after ten years 1 × 1.2 m (3 × 4 ft).

New Zealand flax (*Phormium* species) is a dramatic, spiky-foliaged shrub with a number of particularly attractive forms. *Phormium cookianum* 'Cream Delight' has olive-green leaves with a central cream band; P. *tenax* 'Yellow Wave' has a central yellow band; P.*t.* 'Maori Sunrise' has red-purple leaves with rose-pink and bronze veining; and P.*t.* 'Purpureum' has stiff, broad, bronze-purple leaves. Some varieties do produce flower spikes, but not for several years. In hard winters protect the centre of the plant, from which the new leaves are produced, against frost with bracken or straw. It won't survive in very windy or very cold gardens.

Flowers Jul–Sept. Approx. height and spread after five years 80×80 cm ($2\frac{1}{2} \times 2\frac{1}{2}$ ft); after ten years 1.2×1.5 m (4×5 ft).

Rosemary, like other Mediterranean herbs, loves these conditions too. With its spiky, dark green leaves, and blue flowers in late spring, it makes a good background shrub for the middle of a dry border. Good varieties include *Rosmarinus officinalis*, the smaller *R.o.* 'Benenden blue' and the even smaller *R.o.* 'Severn Sea', which has brilliant blue flowers and reaches about one third the average height and spread.

Flowers May–Jun. Approx. height and spread after five years 80 cm $\times 1$ m ($2\frac{1}{2}$ ft $\times 3$ ft); after ten years 1.2×1.5 m (4×5 ft).

Cotton lavender (*Santolina chamaecyparissus*) is grown for its lovely, delicate, silvery foliage, and though it does produce little, yellow flowers in summer, these not only make the foliage duller but also spoil the shrub's attractive bun shape and so hard pruning in spring is advisable. There is also a green variety, *S. virens*, which has bright green, thread-like foliage – very valuable in providing a contrast to the greys in a dry garden.

Flowers Jun–Aug. Approx. height and spread after five years 50×70 cm ($1\frac{1}{2}$ ft $\times 2$ ft 3 in); after ten years 50 cm $\times 1$ m ($1\frac{1}{2} \times 3$ ft).

Senecio greyii is another attractive grey-leaved foliage shrub which has acid-yellow, daisy flowers in summer. It should be cut back hard in spring to prevent the plant becoming woody and sprawling.

Flowers Jun–Jul. Approx. height and spread after five years 80×80 cm ($2\frac{1}{2} \times 2\frac{1}{2}$ ft); after ten years 1×1 m (3×3 ft).

Spanish broom (*Spartium junceum*), like its fellow brooms, thrives in dry conditions and produces masses of bright yellow, pea-like flowers in midsummer. It dislikes pruning, so if you need to keep its size in check, prune only the current season's growth.

Flowers Jun–Sept. Approx. height and spread after five years 2×1 m (6×3 ft); after ten years 3×2 m (10×6 ft).

Stranvaesia davidiana, like *Photinia* × *fraseri* 'Red Robin', is one of nature's consolation prizes for those without soils acid enough to grow pièris! A semi-evergreen, it has bright red young leaves in spring and small white flowers in early summer, followed by good autumn colour and bright red berries.

Flowers May–Jun. Approx. height and spread after five years 1.5×1.5 m (5×5 ft); after ten years 2.5×2.5 m (8×8 ft).

Yuccas come originally from Mexico, though in fact they'll grow happily in British gardens, given full sun and a dry soil. They are slow-growing, but eventually produce flowers like huge lilies-of-the-valley on spikes up to 2 m (6 ft high). Good varieties include *Yucca filamentosa* and its variegated forms and Y. *gloriosa*, though its leaves are so spiky that it's best not planted where children are likely to run around.

Flowers Jul–Aug. Approx. height and spread after five years 1 × 1m (3 × 3 ft); after ten years 2 × 2 m (6 × 6 ft).

HERBACEOUS PLANTS

Bear's breeches (*Acanthus mollis*) is a tall, striking plant, with spires of curious, purple-hooded, white-rimmed flowers and boldly cut foliage. *A. spinosus* has similar flowers and even more finely cut, positively prickly leaves, while *A. spinosissimus* has leaves so finely cut that they are almost skeletal.

Flowers Jun–Sept. Approx height and spread 1.2 m × 70 cm (4 ft × 2 ft 3 in).

Yarrow (*Achillea* species) is a family with members both small and large which are ideal for dry, sunny conditions. Among the dwarf varieties *Achillea* × 'King Edward', with ferny, green-grey foliage and primrose yellow flowers is good, while among the tall varieties look out for *Achillea* × 'Moonbeam' and 'Moonshine', with greyish foliage and flat heads of bright yellow flowers; *A. millefolium* 'Cerise Queen', with flat heads of intense cerise pink; and, quite different, *A. ptarmica* 'The Pearl', which has pure white, double, button flowers.

Flowers Jun–Aug. Approx. height and spread 10–75 cm × 40–50 cm (4 in–$2\frac{1}{2}$ ft × 16–18 in).

African lily (*Agapanthus* species) has rounded heads of blue or white on long, bare stems riding above clumps of strap-like leaves. Good varieties include *A. campanulatus* 'Albus'; *A.c.* 'Isis', the darkest blue; and Headbourne Hybrids in various shades of blue.

Flowers Jul–Sept. Approx. height and spread 1 m × 70 cm (3 ft × 2 ft 3 in).

Alyssum saxatile is the acid-yellow flowering plant you often see sprawling over a sunny wall next to a bright purple aubretia in late spring/early summer. It has some subtler relatives with grey-green foliage, like *A.s.* 'Citrinum', which has cool lemon flowers, and 'Dudley Neville', with soft apricot-yellow flowers. There's also a variegated form of 'Dudley Neville'.

Flowers Apr–Jun. Approx. height and spread 25 × 25 cm (9 × 9 in).

Ox-eye chamomile (*Anthemis tinctoria*), especially the variety 'E. C. Buxton', with its ferny, green leaves and mass of creamy-yellow daisies carried throughout the summer, is a superb plant for a

The clove-scented pink
(*Dianthus* 'Cantab').

sunny border. The taller 'Wargrave Variety' with cool lemon-yellow flowers is also good.
Flowers Jun–Sept. Approx height and spread 50×30 cm ($1\frac{1}{2} \times 1$ ft).

Artemisias like 'Powys Castle', 'Lambrook Silver' and 'Silver Queen' will also grow well in dry, sunny borders. (See page 151.)

Ballota pseudodictamnus, with its long, curving stems of felty, silver-white, round leaves, revels in dry conditions. It does produce mauve flowers in midsummer, but these are often thought to spoil the effect of the foliage and so are removed. It will die back naturally in all but the mildest winters, and if it doesn't it should be pruned hard to prevent it becoming straggly.
Flowers Jun–Jul. Approx. height and spread 50×60 cm ($1\frac{1}{2} \times 2$ ft).

Convolvulus cneorum is a superb plant with fine, silky, silver leaves with a faint sheen and a succession of ivory trumpets that emerge from long, tightly rolled, rose-pink buds. It is pretty hardy but would benefit from winter protection during its first year.
Flowers Apr–Jul. Approx. height and spread 45×45 cm (17×17 in).

Coreopsis has yellow, daisy-like flowers for a long season in summer. *Coreopsis verticillata* 'Grandiflora' has rich gold daisies, while the new *C.v.* 'Moonbeam' has pale, creamy yellow flowers.
Flowers Jun–Sept. Approx. height and spread 40×30 cm (16 in $\times 1$ ft).

Crocosmia will also thrive in dry conditions. (See page 153.)

Pinks (*Dianthus* species) in their many forms – Chinese pinks, Cheddar pinks, maiden pinks, border pinks or carnations – all love hot, dry, alkaline soils. Of the dwarf varieties look for the mat-forming *Dianthus deltoides* 'Flashing Light' (salmon-red flowers), 'Samos' (carmine) and 'Brighteyes' (red with a white eye), and hybrids like *Dianthus* × 'Little Jock', 'Nyewoods Cream' and 'Pike's Pink'. Of the taller varieties look for allwoodii pinks like the rose-pink 'Doris' and 'Diane', and among the old favourites the double white 'Mrs Sinkins', and any of dozens of new, longer-flowering hybrids like the Devon pinks – *Dianthus* × 'Devon Glow', 'Devon Blush' and 'Devon Cream'.
Flowers Jun–Sept. Approx. height and spread 10–30 cm × 25–75 cm (4 in–1 ft × 10 in–2½ ft).

Globe thistle (*Echinops ritro*) is a striking plant for the back of a border, with prickly, silver-green foliage and steel-blue, round, thistle flowers in late summer.
Flowers Jun–Sept. Approx. height and spread 1.1 m × 70 cm (3 ft 6 in × 2 ft 3 in).

Sea holly (*Eryngium* species) is also a thistle-like plant, only the best of them aren't at all prickly to touch. *E. oliverianum* has deeply cut, green leaves, but its stems and flower heads are all deep blue, while *E. giganteum* 'Miss Willmott's Ghost' – named after the redoubtable Victorian gardener who was said secretly to scatter its seed whenever she visited other people's gardens – has silvery green flowers surrounded by metallic silver, ruffle-like bracts. It's in fact bienniel, but seeds itself freely.
Flowers Jun–Aug. Approx. height and spread 70 × 40 cm (2 ft 3 in × 16 in).

Spurge (*Euphorbia* species) has forms which will also revel in these conditions. The small, prostrate *E. myrsinites* has stems evenly covered in waxy blue leaves, at the end of which are large heads of yellow-green flowers. The larger *E. polychroma* has heads of sulphur-yellow flowers in early summer, while the most spectacular is *E. wulfenii*, which is a large, dramatic, clump-forming plant with tall stems of blue-grey, evergreen leaves topped by large heads of sulphur-yellow flowers.
Flowers Mar–May. Approx. height and spread 15 cm–1.2 m × 30–70 cm (6 in–4 ft × 12 in–2 ft 3 in).

Bronze fennel (*Foeniculum vulgare purpureum*) makes a tall pillar of very fine, bronze, thread-like foliage. It does have yellow flowers in midsummer, but at the expense of more foliage being produced, so many gardeners remove the flower buds. That also prevents the plant from seeding itself everywhere.
Flowers Jul–Oct. Approx height and spread 1.5 m × 60 cm (5 × 2 ft).

Gypsophila, in its dwarf forms, does well on dry soil. (See page 155.)

Rock roses (*Helianthemum* species) are related to the much taller growing *Cistus* species, but these are ground-hugging plants, many with grey foliage, which have white, pink, red, orange or yellow flowers in great profusion throughout the summer. Trimming them after flowering stops them from becoming straggly. Good varieties include the tawny orange-gold 'Ben Nevis', the double red 'Mrs Earle' (also known as 'Fireball'), the red and white 'Raspberry Ripple' and the three 'Wisleys' – pink, primrose and white.
Flowers Jun–Aug. Approx. height and spread 25 × 60 cm (9 in × 2 ft).

Candytuft (*Iberis saxatilis*) is invaluable in the dry, sunny border not only for its chalk-white flowers in spring, but also for its spreading mats of dark green, evergreen foliage.
Flowers Apr–May. Approx. height and spread 8 × 60 cm (3 in × 2 ft).

Rose campion (*Lychnis coronoria*) has downy grey leaves and branching heads of small, intense magenta-pink flowers. There is also a white form. Both seed themselves freely unless they are regularly dead-headed.
Flowers Jun–Sept. Approx. height and spread 60 × 40 cm (2 ft × 16 in).

Catmint (*Nepeta × faassenii* or *N. mussinii*) makes good weed-suppressing clumps of grey-green foliage, with lavender-blue flowers. It gets its common name from the fact that cats love rolling in it. *N. × f.* 'Six Hills Giant' is almost twice the size of its relative, is said to be hardier, and will tolerate a bit more moisture in the soil.
Flowers Apr–Sept. Approx. height and spread 30–60 cm × 30–60 cm (1–2 ft × 1–2 ft).

Evening primrose (*Oenothera missouriensis*) is an excellent choice for the front of a border. It has narrow pointed leaves above which are carried masses of large, trumpet-shaped, lemon flowers from midsummer onwards. They are supposed to open only in the evenings, but they certainly do sometimes open in the daytime.
Flowers Jun–Sept. Approx. height and spread 25 × 45 cm (9 in × 1½ ft).

Sage (*Salvia officinalis*) is another herb invaluable for the dry sunny border. Apart from the ordinary culinary form with its sage-green leaves, there's a variegated cream-and-gold-leafed form, *S.o.* 'Icterina', the purple-leaved form, 'Purpurascens' and the smaller 'Tricolor', variegated in white, pink and purple. The latter need winter protection in cold areas. It has purple-blue flowers in midsummer.
Flowers Jun–Aug. Approx. height and spread 40–60 cm × 40–60 cm (16 in–2 ft × 16 in–2 ft).

Most herbs do best in well-drained soil and full sun.

Ice plant (*Sedum* 'Autumn Joy') is attractive for most of the year, with its low rosettes of fleshy, pale blue-green leaves in spring, which grow through the summer into a mound of foliage. Then the flower stalks appear, carrying large, flat heads of pale green buds which turn slowly from rose pink to salmon and finally, in late autumn, to bronze. You can leave the flower heads on through the winter and when you remove them in early spring you'll find the new rosettes of leaves beneath. Butterflies and bees love this plant. Flowers Aug–Oct. Approx. height and spread 60 × 50 cm (2 ft × 18 in).

Thyme (*Thymus* species) is a marvellous front-of-the-border plant for a hot, dry spot, with flowers ranging from white through pink to mauve. Among the more upright, bushy ones look out for *Thymus × citriodorus* 'Silver Queen', with variegated green and silver leaves, and *T. vulgaris* 'Golden King'. Among the mat-forming ones the dark green-and-gold-variegated *T.* 'Doone Valley', the bright gold *T.* 'Golden Carpet' and the grey-leafed, pink-flowered *T. serpyllum* 'Pink Chintz' are widely available and good. Flowers Jun–Sept. Approx. height and spread 5–30 × 30 cm (2 in–1 ft × 1 ft).

Bouncing Bette (*Saponaria ocymoides*) is a vigorous ground coverer, ideal for a sunny bank, covered in bright pink campion flowers in early summer. It's sometimes sold as a rock plant but its vigour means that it soon smothers other plants in the rock garden. Flowers May–Jul. Approx. height and spread 15 × 75 cm (6 in × 2½ ft).

Lamb's ears (*Stachys lanata*) is another excellent grey-leafed plant whose flowers, with some exceptions, are rather a disadvantage. The form 'Sheila McQueen' has attractive silvery flower spikes, while 'Silver Carpet' is non-flowering, making an excellent carpeter for the front of a border. 'Primrose Heron' is a fine, yellow-leafed variety.
Flowers Jun–Aug. Approx. height and spread 12–30 × 40 cm (5–12 × 16 in).

Mullein (*Verbascum* species) is a stately plant for the back of a border. Apart from the giant *V. olympicum*, which reaches 2 m (6 ft) and more, and has huge woolly, grey-white leaves and stems and clusters of yellow flowers, there are the smaller hybrids like the primrose yellow *Verbascum × hybridum* 'Gainsborough', the rose-pink 'Pink Domino' and the white 'Mont Blanc'.
Flowers Jun–Aug. Approx. height and spread 1.1 m × 40 cm ($3\frac{1}{2}$ ft × 16 in).

Ornamental grasses
Festuca glauca 'Silver Sea' is a compact, powder-blue grass that revels in hot, dry conditions. It's an ideal plant to provide a 'vertical' amid horizontal, mat-forming subjects.
Approx. height and spread 25 × 20 cm (10 × 8 in).

Avena (*Helictotrichon sempervirens*) forms arching clumps of vivid, grey-blue foliage up to 45 cm (18 in) high, with plumes of silvery-grey flowers up to 1.2 m (4 ft) tall in midsummer.
Approx. height and spread 1.2 m × 60 cm (4 × 2 ft).

ANNUALS
Half-hardy annuals best bought as young plants

Gazanias (*Gazania* species) produce large daisy flowers in yellow, orange, pink, and rusty red, some of them single colours, many of them bi-colours. The flowers open only in bright sunshine.
Approx. height 30 cm (12 in).

Livingstone daisies (*Mesembryanthemum* species) also open only in bright sunshine, but they are produced in such numbers that, when they do open, they cover the fleshy, succulent foliage of the plant entirely. They come in glowing shades of pink, carmine, salmon, apricot and gold.
Approx. height 8 cm (3 in).

Hardy annuals to be sown where they are to flower

Star of the veldt (*Dimorphotheca* species) is a sun-loving plant whose flowers actually close when it rains. Among the best varieties

to try are the Aurantiuaca Hybrids, in shades of white, lemon, gold, orange and salmon, or 'Glistening White', whose flowers are described perfectly by their name.
Approx. height 25–30 cm (9–12 in).

California poppy (*Eschscholzia* species) will also put on a dazzling display of red, orange and gold flowers on hot, dry soils. Good varieties include 'Monarch Art Shades', with semi-double flowers, and 'Ballerina', with fluted, double and semi-double flowers in the same range of colours.
Approx. height 25 cm (10 in).

Nasturtiums (*Tropaeolum* species) are invaluable in a dry, sunny situation and as well as being decorative are also edible. Good varieties for small gardens include *T. majus* 'Dwarf Jewel Mixed', which has semi-double flowers in several shades of yellow, orange and deep red, and 'Alaska', which has single flowers in red and orange, set off to perfection by marbled green and white foliage.
Approx. height 25–30 cm (9–12 in).

BULBS
Though many of the traditional, spring-flowering bulbs don't enjoy being baked in summer, some of the more spectacular bulbs enjoy hot, dry conditions.

Ornamental onions (*Allium* species). (See page 163.)

Peruvian lilies (*Alstroemeria* Ligtu Hybrids), with their long stems of small, pink, orange and peach flowers, marked with distinct brown dashes, are becoming increasingly popular as florists' flowers, and are worth trying in a dry, sunny spot, especially if you enrich the soil first with organic matter and mulch them with more of the same once they're planted. They die back after flowering is over, and will need protection in winter.
Flowers Jun–Sept. Approx. height 75 cm ($2\frac{1}{2}$ ft). Plant 30 cm (12 in) apart.

Belladonna lily (*Amaryllis belladonna*) produces stunning, scented, pale satiny-pink lily flowers in early autumn on tall, bare stems (the leaves come later). It's an ideal plant for growing behind a medium-sized shrub that has blue flowers at the same time, like *Ceratostigma willmottianum*.
Flowers Sept–Oct. Approx. height 75 cm ($2\frac{1}{2}$ ft). Plant 30 cm (12 in) apart.

Colchicums. (See page 86.)

Regale lilies (*Lilium regale*). (See page 164.)

Nerines (*Nerine bowdenii*). (See page 165.)

Tulips in the wild grow mainly on sunbaked, rocky hillsides in the Balkans and Central Asia and so do very well in our closest equivalent – limy dry soil in a sunny spot. (See page 165.)

Heavy Clay Soil

CLIMBERS
Ivy (*Hedera* species). (See page 58.)

Wisteria sinensis. (See page 138.)

SHRUBS
Barberry (*Berberis thunbergii*) – gold and purple-leafed forms. (See page 138.)

Japonica (*Chaenomeles speciosa*).
Flowers Jan–Apr. Approx. height and spread 1×2 m (3×5 ft).

Dogwood (*Cornus alba*). (See page 60.)

Woolley willow (*Salix lanata* and *S. hastata* 'Wehrhahnii'). (See page 63.)

Bridal wreath (*Spiraea* × *arguta*). (See page 148.)

Viburnum × burkwoodii and *V. plicatum tomentosum* 'Lanarth'. (See *V.p.* 'Mariesii' page 150.)

Weigela florida. (See page 150.)

HERBACEOUS PLANTS
Bear's breeches (*Acanthus mollis*). (See page 172.)

Japanese anemone (*Anemone* × *hybrida*). (See page 67.)

Michaelmas daisies (*Aster novi-belgii*). (See page 151.)

Crocosmia. (See page 153.)

Foxglove (*Digitalis grandiflora*). (See page 83.)

Helenium autumnale has large daisy-like flowers in shades of red, orange and gold. It needs regular dividing and staking, which makes it a less useful plant in better soil conditions than others that don't. Flowers Aug–Oct. Approx. height and spread 90×50 cm (3 ft $\times 18$ in).

1. *Cistus laurifolius*

2. *Achillea* 'Moonbeam' ×3

30. *Hydrangea petiolaris*

4. *Buddleia* 'Lochinch'

29. *Fremontodendron californicum*

10. *Yucca gloriosa* 'Variegata'

11. *Caryopteris incana* × *mongolica* 'Arthur Simmonds'

17. *Chionodoxa luciliae* ×7

6. *Alyssum saxatile* 'Dudley Neville' ×5

3. *Phormium tenax,* 'Maori Sunrise'

9. *Amaryllis belladonna* ×7

8. *Dianthus* 'Pike's Pink' ×5

5. *Echinops ritro* ×3

12. *Lychnis coronaria* 'Alba' ×3

23. *Berberis thunberg* 'Rose glov'

7. *Santolina virens*

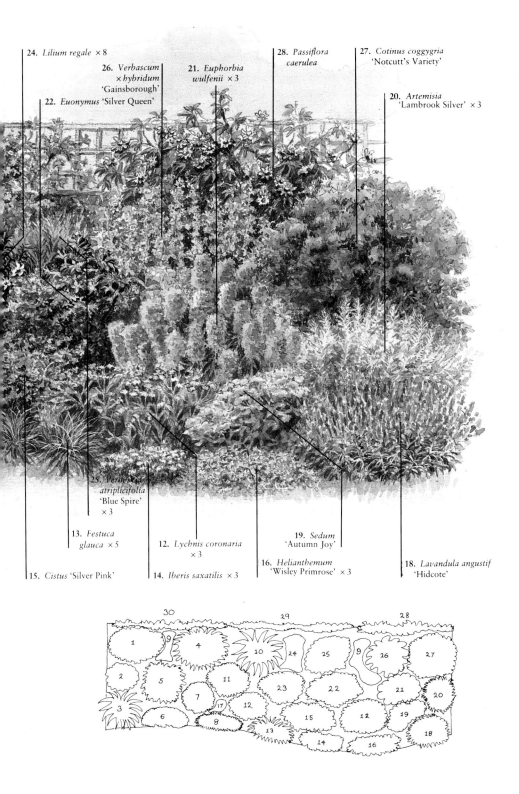

24. *Lilium regale* × 8

26. *Verbascum* × *hybridum* 'Gainsborough'

21. *Euphorbia wulfenii* × 3

28. *Passiflora caerulea*

27. *Cotinus coggygria* 'Notcutt's Variety'

22. *Euonymus* 'Silver Queen'

20. *Artemisia* 'Lambrook Silver' × 3

25. *Perovskia atriplicifolia* 'Blue Spire' × 3

13. *Festuca glauca* × 5

12. *Lychnis coronaria* × 3

19. *Sedum* 'Autumn Joy'

15. *Cistus* 'Silver Pink'

14. *Iberis saxatilis* × 3

16. *Helianthemum* 'Wisley Primrose' × 3

18. *Lavandula angustif* 'Hidcote'

Ligularia dentata. (See page 155.)

Bergamot (*Monarda didyma*). (See page 119.)

Jacob's ladder (*Polemonium caeruleum* and *P. foliosissimum*). (See page 156.)

Knotweed (*Polygonum bistorta* 'Superbum'). (See page 72.)

ANNUALS
Provided you work plenty of organic matter into the soil, most annuals that thrive in sunny, moisture-retentive soil will do well.

BULBS
The vast majority of bulbs rot in heavy clay soils, but it's worth trying some daffodils, like the large-flowered *Narcissus* 'Golden Trumpet', or the much smaller *N*. 'W. P. Milner'.

Planting Plan for a Dry, Sunny Border
(See illus. on pages 180–1.)

CLIMBERS
Allow 3 m (10 ft) for each plant.

1 Climbing hydrangea (*Hydrangea petiolaris*). (See page 58.)

2 *Fremontodendron californicum*. (See page 143.)

3 Passionflower (*Passiflora caerulea*). (See page 138.)

SHRUBS AND TALL PERENNIALS
A Rock rose (*Cistus laurifolius*). One of the tallest and hardiest with white flowers in early summer. (See page 175.)

B *Buddleia* 'Lochinch'. See page 139.)

C *Yucca gloriosa* 'Variegata' is evergreen and, surrounded by deciduous shrubs and climbers, is good in winter. (See page 172.)

D 3 × Russian sage (*Perovskia atriplicifolia* 'Blue Spire'), its blue flowers in late summer contrasting with the bright yellow of the *Fremontodendron*. (See page 170.)

E 3 × mullein (*Verbascum* × *hybridum* 'Gainsborough'), the soft, yellow flowers attractive against the white and purple passionflowers. (See page 177.)

F Smoke bush (*Cotinus coggygria* 'Notcutt's Variety'). (See page 141.)

SMALLER SHRUBS AND PERENNIALS

a 3 × yarrow (*Achillea* 'Moonbeam'). Large, flat heads of clear lemon flowers, attractive against the dark green foliage of the cistus behind. (See page 172.)

b 3 × globe thistle (*Echinops ritro*). Its round, hard blue flower heads good against the long, slender, silver leaves of the buddleia. (See page 174.)

c Cotton lavender (*Santolina virens*). The bright green form provides necessary contrast among the surrounding blue and silver foliage. (See page 171.)

d Blue spiraea (*Caryopteris incana* × *mongolica* 'Arthur Simmonds'). (See page 167.)

e Barberry (*Berberis thunbergii* 'Rose Glow'). Its variegated pink, purple and white leaves blend with the pale grey foliage and blue flowers of the caryopteris on one side and the euphorbia on the other. (See page 139.)

f *Euphorbia wulfenii*. (See page 174.)

g 3 × *Artemisia* 'Lambrook Silver'. Its delicate silver foliage looks superb in front of the deep red cotinus. (See page 151.)

h 3 × rose campion (*Lychnis coronaria* 'Alba'). The branching heads of white flowers are attractive against the caryopteris and the berberis. (See page 175.)

i Spindle (*Euonymus fortunei* 'Silver Queen'). An attractive evergreen. (See page 79.)

j 3 × rose campion (*Lychnis coronaria*). A patch of vivid magenta against the variegated euonymus and the dark green euphorbia. (See page 175.)

k 3 × ice plant (*Sedum* 'Autumn Joy'). Its pale green, fleshy foliage in summer and its pink flower heads in autumn are both attractive against the artemisia. (See page 176.)

l Rock rose (*Cistus* 'Silver Pink'). (See page 169.)

m New Zealand flax (*Phormium tenax* 'Maori Sunrise'). Its deep red, pink and bronze spiky leaves are an interesting contrast in colour and shape to the plants around it. The red also picks up the foliage colour of the berberis and the cotinus in a diagonal line across the border. (See page 170.)

LOW-GROWING SHRUBS AND PERENNIALS

i 5 × *Alyssum saxatile* 'Dudley Neville'. (See page 172.)

ii 5 × pinks (*Dianthus* 'Pike's Pink'). (See page 174.)

iii 5 × *Festuca glauca*. A vertical plant for contrast among the horizontal ones, and attractive against the silver and pink of the cistus. (See page 177.)

iv 3 × candytuft (*Iberis saxatilis*). Another valuable green plant among the greys. Its white flowers in spring are valuable too. (See page 175.)

v 3 × Rock rose (*Helianthemum* 'Wisley Primrose'). (See page 169.)

vi Lavender (*Lavandula angustifolia* 'Hidcote'.) This forms a neat, round bush at the corner of the border. (See page 170.)

BULBS

Aa Belladonna lilies (*Amaryllis belladonna*). (See page 178.)

Bb Regale lilies (*Lilium regale*). (See page 164.)

Cc Glory of the snow (*Chionodoxa luciliae*). (See page 175.)

PLANTS ACCORDING TO THEIR PRIMARY SEASONS OF INTEREST

WINTER

(The following plants are grown for their flowers, bark, catkins, etc. Plants bearing berries, which in some cases last through the winter, are listed under AUTUMN.)

TREES

Acer capillipes (bark). See page 39.
Acer griseum (bark).   See page 39.
Betula jacquemontii (bark). See page 48.
Betula pendula 'Dalecarlica' (bark). See page 48.

Prunus subhirtella 'Autumnalis' (flowers). See page 45.
Salix alba e.g. 'Chermesina' and daphnoides (bark). See page 39.

SHRUBS

Chimonanthus praecox (fragrant flowers). See page 115.
Camellia (flowers). Acid soils only. See page 54.
Cornus alba e.g. 'Westonbirt' and 'Elegantissima' (bark). See page 60.
Daphne odora (fragrant flowers). See page 142.
Erica carnea (flowers). See page 98.
Garyea elliptica (catkins). See page 61.
Hamamelis mollis (fragrant flowers). See page 61.

Jasminum nudiflorum (flowers). See page 79.
Lonicera fragrantissima (fragrant flowers). See page 117.
Mahonia japonica (fragrant flowers). See page 82.
Rhododendron (flowers). Acid soils only. See page 55.
Sarcococca humilis (fragrant flowers). See page 63.
Viburnum × *bodnantense* and *tinus* (fragrant flowers). See page 150.

HERBACEOUS PLANTS

(All grown for their flowers.)
Helleborus niger, orientalis and *foetidus*. See pages 70, 84.

BULBS

(All except *Arum italicum* 'Pictum' grown for their flowers.)
Arum italicum 'Pictum' (variegated leaves). See page 75.
Crocus. See page 164.

Galanthus nivalis. See page 77.
Iris e.g. *reticulata*. See page 164.
Narcissus e.g. 'February Gold' and 'W. P. Milner'. See pages 165, 182.

SPRING

TREES

Acer pseudoplatanus 'Brilliantissimum' (foliage). See page 39.
Amelanchier lamarckii (flowers). See page 49.
Crataegus oxycantha (flowers). See page 40.

Malus floribunda (flowers). See page 41.
Prunus (flowers). See pages 43–6.
Pyrus nivalis and *P. salicifolia* 'Pendula' (foliage). See page 46.

CLIMBERS

Clematis alpina and *macropetala* (flowers). See page 135.

SHRUBS

Berberis darwinii (flowers). See page 78.
Camellia (flowers). See page 54.
Chaenomeles (flowers). See page 179.
Corylopsis pauciflora (flowers). See page 134.
Daphne mezereum (fragrant flowers). See page 142.
Magnolia stellata (flowers). See page 146.
Osmanthus delavayi (fragrant flowers). See page 146.
Pachysandra terminalis (flowers). See page 62.
Pieris (foliage and flowers). Acid soils only.
  See page 55.

Rhododendrons/azaleas (flowers). Acid soils only.
  See pages 55–7.
Ribes sanguineum (flowers). See page 82.
Salix hastata 'Wehrhahnii' (catkins). See page 63.
Spiraea × arguta (flowers). See page 148.
Viburnum burkwoodii, carlesii and *juddii* (fragrant
  flowers). See page 118.
Vinca major and *minor* (flowers). See pages 82–3.

HERBACEOUS PLANTS

(All grown for their flowers except where stated.)
Alyssum saxatile. See page 172.
Bergenia. See page 70.
Dicentra spectabilis. See page 70.
Epimedium. See page 84.
Euphorbia polychroma. See page 107.

Iberis saxatilis. See page 175.
Lamium. See page 71.
Polygonatum. See page 72.
Primula. See page 73.
Pulmonaria saccharata. See page 73.
Waldsteinia ternata. See page 86.

BULBS

Anemone blanda and *nemorosa*. See page 163.
Chionodoxa luciliae. See page 75.
Crocus. See page 164.
Erythronium dens-canis. See page 76.
Leucojum vernum. See page 77.

Muscari. See page 77.
Narcissus. See page 165.
Ornithogalum. See pages 87, 165.
Tulips. See page 165.

SUMMER

(Since there are so many flowering plants in this category, they are subdivided into 'Early'
(May–July) and 'Late' (July–Sept.). Those that aren't marked flower all summer.)

TREES

Laburnum × watereri 'Vossii' (flowers). See page 40.
Malus e.g. 'Liset', 'Red Jade' and *sargentii*.
  See pages 41–2.

Prunus e.g. 'Kanzan' and *serrula*. See pages 43, 44.
Sorbus e.g. *cashmiriana* and *vilmorinii*. See page 47.

CLIMBERS

Campsis radicans. Late. See page 135.
Clematis – Early include *montana*, 'Nelly Moser', 'Mrs
  Cholmondeley', 'Marie Boisselot'. Late include
  'Jackmanii', *texensis* and *viticella*. See pages 57,
  135.
Eccremocarpus scaber. Late. See page 136.
Fremontodendron californicum. See page 143.
Hydrangea petiolaris. Early. See page 58.
Lonicera – *japonica*, 'Halliana'. Early include

periclymenum 'Belgica' and *americana*. Late
include *periclymenum* 'Serotina', *heckrotii*
'Goldflame', 'Dropmore Scarlet', and
tellmanniana. See pages 58, 114.
Passiflora. See page 138.
Roses. Most ramblers flower early. Repeat-flowering
climbers flower all summer. See page 138.
Solanum crispum. Late. See page 138.
Wisteria. Early. See page 138.

SHRUBS

Berberis. Early. See page 78.

Buddleia davidii, fallowiana and 'Lochinch'. Late. See page 139.

Carpenteria californica. Early. See page 140.

Caryopteris incana. Late. See page 167.

Ceanothus. Evergreens early, deciduous varieties late. See page 140.

Ceratostigma willmottianum. Late. See page 140.

Cistus. Early. See page 169.

Convolvulus cneorum. Early. See page 173.

Cytisus (including *battandieri*). Early. See pages 136, 142.

Escallonia. Early (except 'Iveyi'). See page 142.

Fuchsia. Late. See page 98.

Hebe. Some early – e.g. *elliptica* 'Variegata' and 'Carl Teschner'. Some late – e.g. 'Autumn Glory', 'Great Orme' and 'Midsummer Beauty'. See page 143.

Hydrangea. Early – *paniculata*. Late – lace-caps and mop-heads. See page 62.

Hypericum patulum 'Hidcote'. Late. See page 143.

Itea ilicifolia. Late. See page 134.

Kalmia latifolia. Early. Acid soils only. See page 134.

Kolkwitzia amabilis. Early. See page 143.

Lavender. Late. See page 170.

Myrtus communis. Late. See page 117.

Perovskia. Late. See page 170.

Philadelphus. Early. See page 146.

Pieris. Early. Acid soils only. See page 55.

Potentilla fruticosa. See page 146.

Prunus laurocerasus e.g. 'Otto Luyken'. Early. See page 82.

Pyracantha. Early. See page 62.

Rhododendrons/azaleas. Early. Acid soils only. See pages 55–7.

Romneya. Late. See page 147.

Roses. See page 147.

Skimmia. Early. See page 63.

Spiraea. Late – *bumalda* and *japonica*. See page 148.

Syringa. Early (*S. microphylla* 'Superba' also Late). See pages 148–50.

Viburnum – e.g. *opulus* and *plicatum*. Early. See page 150.

Weigela florida. Early. See page 150.

HERBACEOUS PLANTS

Since the vast majority of herbaceous plants flower in the summer, and their flowering period has already been given in their descriptions in the different chapters, it seems pointless to list them all again. So unless a herbaceous plant is listed under WINTER, SPRING, or AUTUMN, you can safely assume it flowers in summer.

ANNUALS

All annuals flower in summer.

BULBS

Allium. Early–mid summer. See page 163.

Amaryllis belladonna. Late summer–early autumn. See page 178.

Galtonia candicans. Late summer. See page 164.

Lilies. Mid–late summer. See page 164.

AUTUMN

(Plants grown mainly for berries, or autumn foliage colour.)

TREES

Acer griseum (autumn foliage colour). See page 39.

Amelanchier lamarckii (autumn foliage colour). See page 49.

Cercidiphyllum japonicum (autumn foliage colour). See page 50.

Malus – e.g. 'John Downie' (the best 'crabs' of all), 'Golden Hornet'. 'Red Jade', 'Royalty' (berries). See pages 42, 43.

Prunus e.g. *sargentii*, and *yedoensis* (autumn foliage colour). See pages 44, 46.

Sorbus e.g. 'Joseph Rock', 'Embley', *cashmiriana* and *vilmorinii* (autumn foliage colour and berries). See pages 46–7.

CLIMBERS

Clematis orientalis (flowers and seed heads). See page 135.

Parthenocissus e.g. henryana (autumn foliage colour). See page 59.

SHRUBS

Acer palmatum dissectum (autumn foliage colour). See page 59.

Aucuba japonica (berries). See page 59.

Berberis. Berries and some, like B. thunbergii, autumn foliage colour. See page 78.

Cotinus coggygria (autumn foliage colour). See page 141.

Cotoneaster. Berries and some, like C. horizontalis, autumn foliage colour. See page 141.

Gautheria procumbens. Acid soils only. Berries. See page 54.

Ilex. Berries. See page 79.

Pernettya mucronata. Acid soils only. Berries. See page 55.

Pyracantha (berries). See page 62.

Rhus typhina (autumn foliage colour). See page 82.

Skimmia (berries). See page 63.

Stranvaesia (berries). See page 171.

Viburnum – davidii and opulus berries. V. opulus also autumn foliage colour. See pages 66, 150.

HERBACEOUS PLANTS

(Many late summer-flowering plants will still be flowering.)

Anemone × hybrida. See page 67.

Aster amellis, novae-angliae and novi-belgii. See pages 151, 179.

Cimicifuga. See page 70.

Crocosmia. See page 153.

Kniphofia. See page 155.

Rudbeckia. See page 157.

Schizostylis coccinea. See page 158.

Sedum 'Autumn Joy'. See page 176.

BULBS

Autumn crocus. See page 110.

Colchicums. See page 86.

Cyclamen hederifolium. See page 76.

Nerine bowdenii. See page 165.

SPECIALIST NURSERIES

TREES AND SHRUBS
Hilliers, Ampfield House, Ampfield Romsey, Hants. Catalogue £1.

Notcutts Nurseries, Woodbridge, Suffolk IP12 4AF. Catalogue £2.70.

CLEMATIS
Fisk's Clematis Nursery, Westleton, nr Saxmundham, Suffolk IP17 3AJ.

Treasures of Tenbury, Burford House, Tenbury, Wells WR15 8HQ. Catalogue £1.60.

DWARF CONIFERS
Bressingham Gardens, Diss, Norfolk IP22 2AB. Catalogue £1.50.

RHODODENDRONS AND AZALEAS
Hydon Nurseries, Clock Barn Lane, Hydon Heath, Godalming, Surrey. Catalogue £1.50.

G. Reuthe, Branch Nursery, Crown Point, Ightham, nr Sevenoaks, Kent. Catalogue 70p.

VARIEGATED/COLOURED FOLIAGE PLANTS
Hoecroft Plants, Fosse Lane, Welton, Midsomer Norton, Bath, Avon. Catalogue 85p.

ROSES
David Austin Roses, Bowling Green Lane, Albrighton, Wolverhampton WV7 3HB. New 'old roses'. Catalogue 75p.

Harkness Roses, The Rose Gardens, Hitchen, Herts. SG4 0JT. Catalogue free.

HARDY PERENNIALS
Unusual Plants, Beth Chatto Gardens, White Barn House, Elmstead Market, nr Colchester, Essex. Catalogue £1.30.

Plants from a Country Garden, The Thatched Cottage, Duck Lane, Ludgershall, Aylesbury, Bucks HP18 9NZ. Catalogue 3 × 14p stamps.

SILVER LEAFED PLANTS
Ramparts Nurseries, Baker's Lane, Braiswick, nr Colchester, Essex CO4 5BB. Catalogue, 2 × 19p stamps.

GROUND COVER PLANTS
Growing Carpets, The Old Farmhouse, Steeple Morden, nr Royston, Herts SG8 0PP. Catalogue 64p.

ALPINES
W. E. Th. Ingwersen, Birch Farm Nursery, Gravetye, East Grinstead, W. Sussex RH19 4LE. Catalogue £1.

Hartside Nursery Garden, Low Gill Hou Alston, Cumbria CA9 3BL. Catalogue 3 × 14p stamps.

DELPHINIUMS AND BEGONIAS
Blackmore & Langdon, Pensford, Bristo BS18 4JL. Catalogue 1 × 19p stamp.

HELLEBORES (AND SNOWDROPS)
Helen Ballard, Old Country, Mathon, Malvern, Hereford and Worcester WR13 5PS. Send SAE for plant list.

PAEONIES AND IRIS
Kelways, Langport, Somerset TA10 9SL. Catalogue 2 × 19p stamps.

BULBS
Walter Blom and Sons, Coombelands Nurseries, Leavesden, Watford WD2 7BI Catalogues free.

Broadleigh Gardens, Barr House, Bishop Hull, Taunton, Somerset TA4 1AE. Catalogue 2 × 19p stamps.

SEEDS
Dobies, Unit B, Broomhill Way, Torqua Devon TQ2 7QJ. Catalogue free.

Mr Fothergill's Seeds, Grazeley Road, Kentford, Newmarket, Suffolk CB8 7QB Catalogue free.

Index

PICTURE CREDITS